# The Tempest

A PRACTICAL GUIDE FOR TEACHING SHAKESPEARE
IN THE MIDDLE GRADE CLASSROOM

Retold by Christine Hood & Lori Cardoza-Starnes

Illustrated by Robin DeWitt & Patricia Grush

Project Director: Mina McMullin

Senior Editor: Christine Hood

Contributing Writer: Alain Chirinian

Inside and Cover Design: Rita Hudson

Cover Illustration: Robin DeWitt

GOOD APPLE
A Division of Frank Schaffer Publications
23740 Hawthorne Blvd.
Torrance, CA 90505

© 1998 Good Apple. All rights reserved. Printed in the United States of America.

**Notice!** Pages may be reproduced for classroom or home use only, not for commercial resale. No part of this publication may be reproduced for storage in a retrieval system, or transmitted in any form or by any means—electronic, mechanical, recording, etc.—without the prior written permission of the publisher. Reproduction of these materials for an entire school or school system is strictly prohibited.

# Contents

Introduction .................................................................... 4

The Life and Times of William Shakespeare ........................ 5

The Elizabethan Stage ..................................................... 7

About *The Tempest* ......................................................... 9

*The Tempest* Summary .................................................... 11

Cast of Characters ......................................................... 16

*The Tempest* ................................................................. 17

Vocabulary ................................................................... 45

Introducing Drama ........................................................ 47

The Language of Shakespeare ......................................... 48

Let's Put on a Play! ....................................................... 49

Journal/Discussion Topics .............................................. 52

Extension Activities ...................................................... 57

References ................................................................... 64

# Introduction

If you asked 100 people to name the greatest writer in history, most of them would probably say, *William Shakespeare.* Shakespeare, a cultural icon of the English-speaking world, has been revered throughout history for his extraordinary skill with language; his unforgettable characters; and his wonderful, many-faceted stories. Some people have been led to believe that Shakespeare is difficult to understand or just not relevant to today's world. Unfortunately, many students' first exposure to Shakespeare may be sitting in a classroom passively listening to the teacher lecture or analyzing passages that seem to have no meaning or relevance to their lives. Studying Shakespeare should not be a "passive" experience; rather, it should be exciting, stimulating, and most of all, fun! It is for this reason that this book was created.

When students are drawn into the humanity of Shakespeare's work, they see how it relates to their lives and the world around them. His themes are central to the struggles and triumphs of humankind; his characters highlight the strength, passion, and joy of humanity as well as its darker, more malevolent side. Although the settings of his stories are in faraway times and places, they deal with contemporary topics. Shakespeare wrote of people in the depths of despair, the throes of comic madness, diabolical plotting, scheming, wooing, and "lovemaking." This may sound like the stuff of soap operas, movies, or TV sitcoms, but that is exactly why students will relate to Shakespeare—a writer for all ages.

In order for students to truly enjoy and appreciate Shakespeare, they shouldn't just read his work, but rather, "experience" it. Before beginning a play study, introduce Shakespeare as a person. Where was he born? What do we know about his life? his family? What was England like during Shakespeare's time? Were his plays as popular then as they are today? What was the life of an actor and playwright like in Elizabethan England? Answering these and other questions for students gives them a personal and historical perspective on Shakespeare and the Elizabethan stage, complementing their overall understanding and enjoyment of his plays.

This book contains a simple summary and an edited version of the play *The Tempest*, in which some language has been simplified for easier student understanding. It also provides suggestions for performing the play; a comprehensive vocabulary list; journal/discussion topics; and a myriad of activities that draw students into the plot, characters, and meaning of the story. These activities will help develop children's imaginations; language and critical-thinking skills; and creative expression through writing, dramatic presentation, and art.

If students' first encounter with Shakespeare is a positive one, they will be "turned on" to future experiences. Learning that "old" doesn't necessarily mean "old-fashioned" opens not only Shakespeare's world to students, but also that of other classic writers and artists.

# The Life and Times of William Shakespeare

Shakespeare's plays do not reveal much about him as a person. Since the plots are so varied and deal with a myriad of social and political issues, Shakespeare's actual views remain elusive and mysterious.

Shakespeare's birthday is recognized as April 23, 1564. He was born in the small English town of Stratford-upon-Avon. The town's name developed because Stratford was nestled next to the River Avon. Shakespeare's father, John, was a successful Stratford glove maker who dealt in leather goods; and his mother, Mary Arden, came from a wealthy Catholic family.

Not much is known about Shakespeare until his marriage to Anne Hathaway in 1582. He was 18 and she was 26. During their marriage, they had three children—Susanna, born in 1583, and the twins Judith and Hamnet, born in 1585.

From 1585 to 1592, no official records exist on Shakespeare. But by the age of 28, he had moved to London and become an actor with a small company of players. Even as he became a successful playwright, he continued to act in his own and others' plays. Between 1589 and 1594, Shakespeare's first plays, *Henry VI*, *Titus Andronicus*, and *The Comedy of Errors*, were a huge success in the London theatre circuit. Shakespeare soon made a name for himself and attained instant popularity.

London was a very exciting place during Shakespeare's time. Elizabeth I was queen when he began his career. English ships ruled the seas, and English explorers were claiming territories as far away as America and the Far East. Shakespeare incorporated much of the excitement, mystery, and adventure of this time period into his work. Unfortunately, in the early 1590s, the plague in London led to the closing of all the theatres. During this time, Shakespeare began writing poetry, including his famous sonnets. This poetry demonstrates Shakespeare's true artistic skill with verse.

When the theatres reopened around 1594, Shakespeare helped form the acting company known as the Lord Chamberlain's Men. For the next ten years, it was London's most popular acting company. The company also started its own theatre—the Globe—and Shakespeare became the primary shareholder. The Globe became a popular entertainment spot for both commoners and wealthy aristocrats.

Shakespeare's greatest writing occurred between 1599 and 1608. During this time, he wrote such popular plays as *Twelfth Night*, *Hamlet*, *Macbeth*, and *Othello*. In 1603, with the succession of James I, Shakespeare's company received a royal patent, and they changed their name to the King's Men. They were then able to perform at the royal court several times a year.

Between 1610 and 1611, Shakespeare retired to his home in Stratford. Here he collaborated with John Fletcher on three more plays—*Henry VIII*, *The Two Noble Kinsmen*, and *Cardenio*.

In 1616, Shakespeare died at the young age of 52. Records show that he was buried on April 25, so it's assumed he died on April 23, two days earlier. This date has been suspect since it is also his birthday. No one knows how Shakespeare died, so his death remains shrouded in mystery. Over 20 possible causes of death have been speculated, including writer's cramp, too much alcohol, and murder.

Regardless of what brought Shakespeare to his demise, his incredible life left humankind a prolific treasure in his writings. Shakespeare wrote 37 plays, 154 sonnets, and two narrative poems. His plays fall into three categories: histories such as *Richard III* and *Henry V*, tragedies such as *Macbeth* and *Othello*, and comedies such as *Twelfth Night* and *As You Like It*.

Shakespeare's deep understanding of human nature and his incredible talent for making characters realistic and human make his work uniquely great. Most aspects of human nature haven't changed much from Elizabethan England. One may even find something of him- or herself or a friend in one of Shakespeare's characters. Much as they did in Elizabethan England, these plays can still move audiences to tears or make them roar with laughter. It is these timeless qualities that keep Shakespeare at the top of the literary and theatrical world.

# The Elizabethan Stage

Theatre was an entirely different experience for the Elizabethans than it is for audiences today. The stage was round, so the audience was highly involved in the performance. Actors sometimes spoke to the audience through soliloquies and asides, and audience members often answered back. Elizabethan theatregoers yelled, laughed, taunted, talked, and ate throughout the performance.

During the Elizabethan period, politicians and clergy were opposed to the theatre, claiming it was a dangerous diversion from religion. So, playhouses were banned in London's city proper and forced out to the suburbs in an area known as Southwark. In this "theatre district," patrons could choose between nine different theatres. Strewn among the theatres were pubs, taverns, and bawdy houses as well as pickpockets and thieves, which only added to the theatre's already bad reputation.

When a play was about to begin, it was a announced with a raised flag and a trumpeted fanfare. The flag indicated the theme of that day's play—black for tragedy, white for comedy, and red for history. When patrons entered a theatre for a performance, they placed their admission money in a box (or "box office"). They could sit in the "galleries" on wooden benches, on cushions in front of the stage, on the stage itself (for more money), or stand in back with the crowd. The general "mob scene" of the crowd (known as "groundlings") created quite a spectacle. Since few Elizabethans bathed, the theatres smelled of sweat, beer, and garlic. It's no wonder the groundlings were also referred to as "penny stinkards." Vendors sold beer, fruit, and nuts, and in the often tumultuous, rowdy atmosphere of a play, these snacks would sometimes be thrown at the actors onstage.

Like all other playhouses, Shakespeare's Globe was under the patronage of a nobleman.

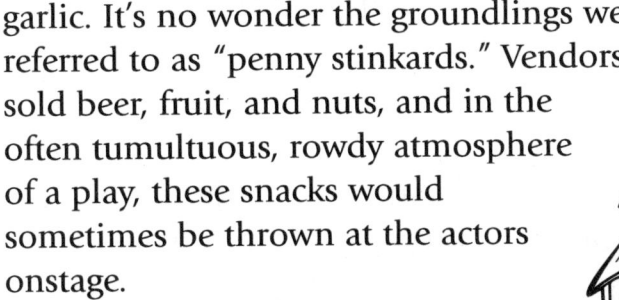

This patronage provided protection from the Puritans as well as additional financial backing. Shakespeare's company was originally "attached" to Lord Chamberlain, and later to James I, becoming the most prestigious theatre company in London.

Shakespeare wrote specifically for his stage in the Globe. Often referred to as a "wooden O," the Globe may have had as many as 20 sides to provide its circular appearance. The theatre was open to the outside and could hold close to 3,000 people. The stage consisted of three tiers—"heaven," "earth," and "hell." A trapdoor in the main stage, or "earth," was used to raise and lower actors and props into and out of "hell." The canopy over the stage was painted with golden stars to represent the "heavens." Often, pulleys and ropes lowered or raised actors up to and from "heaven." A hut on top of the canopy housed props for sound effects such as thunder and cannon fire. Audiences hooted and hollered with delight when such special stage and sound effects were used.

Unlike plays and movies today, scenery and props were limited. To let the audience know what time of day it was or what the weather was like, it was described with an actor's words. For example, when Romeo and Juliet awaken in her chamber, we know it is morning when Romeo says, "It was the lark, the herald of the morn . . . Look, love, what envious streaks do lace the severing clouds in yonder east." Actors also wore elaborate, gaudy costumes and makeup, which were considered sinful by the clergy.

During this time, women were not allowed to act on the public stage, so young boys played the female roles. That is one reason why there are so few women characters in Shakespeare's plays. Not being able to rely on "traditional" feminine beauty for his female characters, Shakespeare created those with amazing intelligence and wit.

Theatres put on a great variety of plays every season. In six months, one company might give about 150 performances of 25 to 30 different plays. Given the quick turnover, rehearsal time was extremely short. Actors only had about a week to learn their parts—up to 800 lines a day for leading roles!

Unfortunately, Shakespeare's revered Globe Theatre burned down in 1613 during a performance of *Henry VIII*. A prop cannon exploded and set the theatre aflame. The theatre was eventually rebuilt, but in 1642, the Puritans finally got their way. The English Parliament passed an ordinance shutting down all theatres, and as a result, the Globe was destroyed in 1644.

# About *The Tempest*

*The Tempest* was written near the end of Shakespeare's career as a playwright and is seen by some as his "farewell" to the stage. Often referred to as a tragicomedy, *The Tempest* doesn't fit easily into any particular category (such as comedy, tragedy, or history). A tragicomedy is a play with a happy ending, but also includes tragic elements that could end unhappily. *The Tempest* fits this description in that it deals with various serious issues such as Caliban's attempted assault on Miranda; the murder plots against Alonso, Gonzalo, and Prospero; and the "colonialism" of Prospero, who takes over an island and claims it as his own while enslaving Caliban and Ariel, two of the island's original inhabitants. On the comic side, the story includes love, magic, charms, humor, and of course, a happy ending with the marriage of Miranda and Ferdinand, and Prospero reclaiming his dukedom.

Several themes run throughout the play, including ideas of reconciliation and forgiveness. Forgiveness permeates almost every aspect and character in the play, as Prospero forgives Alonso, Sebastian, and Antonio; Caliban forgives Prospero; Prospero forgives Caliban; and even Ariel, at first enslaved by Prospero, harbors no bitterness and is merely thankful for his release. As is often demonstrated in Shakespeare's plays, the union of a younger generation (Ferdinand and Miranda) makes up for the "sins" of the older generation. Through the marriage of this couple, Prospero and Alonso are reconciled. Shakespeare shows us that goodness and love can conquer evil.

Another central theme in the play is the contrast between nature and civilization. This theme is played out through the character of Caliban, who is the epitome of the natural, uncivilized world. In fact, the name *Caliban* is thought to be an anagram of "cannibal." In Elizabethan England, civilization, or society, was believed to have been divinely created, and those outside this "civilized" world were considered beastly. In his creation of Caliban, Shakespeare may have been thinking of an essay called "Of Cannibals" written by French philosopher

Montaigne. This essay disputed the Renaissance belief that society was "good," and everything outside of it "bad." Out of this idea sprouted the theory of the "noble savage," which stated that man was purer in nature than when "corrupted" by society. Caliban is the essence of the noble savage, a demi-monster who lived in communion with nature until Prospero attempted to "civilize" and then eventually enslave him. Prospero, on the other hand, represents the reason and control of society. This sounds much like the familiar story of early Europeans who came to the "new world," claiming its land and attempting to "civilize" the Native Americans.

We see this parallel when Caliban describes his first interactions with Prospero. He claims, "I loved thee; and I showed thee all the qualities of the island." He showed Prospero how to survive and how to make the most of his new home. Prospero, who pitied Caliban as a common "beast," attempted to "civilize" him by teaching him his language and educating him as he would a European. When Prospero points this out, Caliban responds angrily, "You taught me language. And my profit on it is, I know how to curse!" Prospero views Caliban as "a born monster, on whose nature nurture can never stick." He feels this way simply because Caliban will not abide by his ways, the ways of society. Some see Caliban as a tormented beast, who coexisted with nature harmoniously before Prospero tried to change him. We question Caliban's nature when we learn of his attack on Miranda, but in light of his torment, we can also understand his need to "people" the island with more of his kind.

Gonzalo further emphasizes this "nature vs. civilization" theme when he describes his idea of the perfect society, in which "nature should bring forth, of its own kind, all abundance." He would allow no monarchy, no magistrate, and no occupation, and claims that "all men would be idle . . . innocent and pure." Gonzalo rejects the Renaissance view of civilization, and would rather see mankind existing harmoniously with nature, which would provide everything they needed to survive.

Many believe *The Tempest* to be Shakespeare's farewell to the stage. In the character of Prospero he seems to have created himself. At the end of the play, Prospero says, "But this rough magic I here give up . . . I'll break my staff, bury it in the earth, and drown my books in the sea." This could very well have been Shakespeare saying he was giving up playwriting. He will break his staff (pen) so he can no longer create magic (plays and poetry). *The Tempest* combines many elements from other plays—tragedy, murder, love, magic, forgiveness—into one. And this culmination is the perfect end to Shakespeare's prolific career.

# The Tempest
## Summary

### ❦ ACT ONE ❦

The story begins as a ship bound for Naples is tossed on the sea during a terrific storm. Onboard are the king of Naples, Alonso; his son Ferdinand; his brother Sebastian; the duke of Milan, Antonio; his loyal counselor Gonzalo; and many others. The ship finally wrecks upon the waves, throwing all its passengers into the sea. As it turns out, this storm, or tempest, has been created through the magic of Prospero, who watches the ship from the shore of a nearby island. For twelve years, Prospero and his daughter Miranda have been living on this island, trying their best to survive. As he and his daughter watch the storm together, Prospero explains how and why they came to be there.

Twelve years ago, he relates, he had been the duke of Milan—a powerful man—and she, a princess. At that time, he became obsessively involved with studying magic and the liberal arts. So obsessed, in fact, that he left the government in the hands of his brother Antonio. Antonio's ambition drove him to plot with the king of Naples against Prospero. In exchange for his help in removing Prospero from power, Antonio would pay the king twice the taxes Prospero had. Antonio would then get rid of Prospero and replace him as duke of Milan. Alonso and Antonio hired henchmen to set Prospero and his three-year-old daughter out to sea in the rotting carcass of a boat. Gonzalo, one of Prospero's loyal counselors, stocked the boat with food, clothes, Prospero's beloved books, and various necessities. To him they owed their survival. Soon he and Miranda landed

on this mystical island, where Prospero had spent the last twelve years tutoring her and studying magic.

When Miranda voices concern about those on the wrecked ship, Prospero explains that, much to his luck, these passengers are the very enemies who set them adrift back in Italy. He himself has caused this storm so he can revenge himself upon them. He casts a spell over Miranda, causing her to fall asleep, and then summons Ariel, one of the island's spirits, who he has under his power. Ariel has dutifully done all Prospero has commanded and reminds Prospero of his promise to set him free. Prospero then recalls how he saved Ariel when first coming to the island. Ariel was imprisoned by Sycorax, a cruel witch who gave birth to a half-man, half-beast son, Caliban. After Sycorax's death, Prospero released Ariel from bondage and took Caliban into his home as a student. Several years later, Caliban became rebellious and tried to attack Miranda, hoping to "populate the island with Calibans." Prospero angrily imprisoned Caliban in a rock and used him as a slave.

Prospero promises to set Ariel free if he remains dutiful for a while longer, and then instructs him to use his magic to lure the king's son, Ferdinand. Prospero awakens his daughter just in time for her to see the approaching Ferdinand, who appears spellbound by Ariel's music.

"I might call him a thing divine," Miranda breathes upon seeing this handsome man. "For nothing natural I ever saw so noble." Ferdinand and Miranda are instantly love-struck. This pleases Prospero, for it is part of his plan. He knows Ferdinand is the king's son, and he wants his daughter to eventually marry him so they will reign together in Naples. When he sees how interested they are in each other, he decides to test Ferdinand's love. "This swift business I must make uneasy, lest too light winning make the prize light," Prospero thinks. He pretends to distrust Ferdinand and accuses him of being a spy. He threatens to put Ferdinand in chains, and when Ferdinand resists, he casts a spell on him so that he cannot move. Ferdinand finally agrees to go with Prospero in hopes that he can still look upon the fair Miranda.

## ⚜ ACT TWO ⚜

On another part of the island, the survivors of the shipwreck mourn the supposed loss Ferdinand. While they rest, Gonzalo muses about his ideal society, if he could make one on the island—no one would need weapons, and no one would work. Nature would provide all the necessities of life. As he speaks, Sebastian and Antonio mock him as a old fool.

Under Prospero's command, Ariel casts a spell on all of them except Sebastian and Antonio, causing them to fall asleep. As they sleep, Antonio and

Sebastian plot the king's death so Sebastian can take the throne. As they raise their swords to strike, Ariel sings in Gonzalo's ear, causing him to wake up. When questioned why their swords are drawn, Sebastian and Antonio claim to have heard a lion roaring in the brush. Alonso asks them to be careful of the beast, but to continue searching for Ferdinand.

Meanwhile, on another part of the island, Caliban collects wood under Prospero's command. He curses Prospero, claiming he is a tyrant and a sorcerer. Caliban believes himself to be the rightful owner of the island, since he was there first, and that Prospero has stolen it from him. Suddenly, Trinculo, the king's jester, stumbles upon Caliban. "What have we here? A man or a fish?" Trinculo ponders, peering at the monster who has fallen to the ground in fear. Soon Stephano, the king's butler, appears holding a jug of wine. He has been drinking heavily and gives some to Trinculo and Caliban as well. Caliban is convinced that Stephano and his "celestial liquor" are from the gods. He falls to his knees in worship before Stephano, vowing to give him the island if he will help him kill Prospero. Caliban also promises that Prospero's beautiful daughter, Miranda, will become Stephano's wife. Stephano, thinking all others from the ship drowned, decides he would like to rule on this island. He and Trinculo agree to the plot. Little do they know that Ariel has witnessed the entire scene. Ariel quickly flies back to inform his master, Prospero, of the evil murder plot.

## ⚜ ACT THREE ⚜

In the woods near Prospero's home, Ferdinand hauls logs while Miranda watches and weeps for him. Prospero makes himself invisible and stands by, observing their interaction. Upon seeing Miranda's tears, Ferdinand comforts her, saying, "This base task would be burdensome to me, but the mistress I serve makes my labors pleasures." She offers to help him, but he refuses. "Do you love me?" Miranda asks, and Ferdinand replies that he loves and prizes her more than the world. Innocent of society's "rules" and expectations regarding courting and love, Miranda asks Ferdinand if he will marry her. He eagerly accepts her offer. Prospero is most joyful at their union, yet knows he must still deal with his enemies.

Weary from searching the island, the king and his followers decide to rest a while. Prospero and Ariel then arrive on the scene, invisible. Using his magic, Prospero conjures several spirits, who present the men with a sumptuous and elaborate banquet. The spirits dance about the table and invite the hungry men to eat. As they are about to partake of the feast, thunder booms and lightning flashes. Ariel appears in the form of a harpy, wings flapping wildly over the table. The men stand terrified as Ariel curses them for their crimes against Prospero. Ariel then calls upon the spirits to carry away the banquet table and casts a spell of madness upon Alonso, Sebastian, and Antonio. Pleased with Ariel's performance, Prospero returns home to Ferdinand and Miranda.

## ACT FOUR

Prospero celebrates Miranda's and Ferdinand's engagement with an elaborate feast. He calls upon the spirits to entertain them with dancing, singing, and music. As they watch, Prospero suddenly remembers that Caliban and his conspirators are on their way to murder him. Ariel tells Prospero that he has lured them into a stinking lake near Prospero's home and set out beautiful garments and trinkets as bait to trick them into thievery. This way, Prospero can prove their treachery and expose their plot.

As soon as the three rogues see the "bait" Ariel displayed, Trinculo and Stephano greedily steal everything they can lay their hands on. However, Caliban urges them to ignore their new-found treasures and murder Prospero first. He worries that Prospero may awaken and find them, thus ruining their plan. Prospero calls upon the spirits to appear as hounds to drive away the thieves. Ariel and Prospero spur on the hounds as they chase the would-be murderers away.

## ACT FIVE

Ariel informs Prospero that he has kept the king and his group in a state of madness in a nearby grove of trees. As Prospero puts on his magical robes, he instructs Ariel to bring the men to him. He will restore the men to their right minds as his last act of magic. He then vows to break his staff and bury it in the ground, and drown his magic books in the sea.

Ariel brings the men into a magic circle Prospero has formed. They slowly regain their senses as Prospero addresses their crimes. First, he praises Gonzalo, claiming he will "repay his loyalties, both in word and deed." He then turns to Alonso and Sebastian, reminding them of their cruelty to him and his daughter. "My flesh and blood, my brother," he says, turning to Antonio, "whose ambition replaced your good nature, who with Sebastian here would have killed your king; I do forgive thee." Having fully regained their reason, the men stand amazed to see Prospero before them. Prospero then quietly tells Sebastian and Antonio that he knows about their plot against the king, but will not expose them as traitors. He forgives them outright for their crimes.

Most graciously, Prospero embraces Alonso and welcomes them to the island. In response, Alonso returns the rightful dukedom to Prospero and begs his forgiveness. With an open heart, Prospero forgives them all and promises to relate the details of his survival on the island. Alonso then sorrowfully tells Prospero about losing his son Ferdinand in the tempest.

"As great to me, for I have lost my daughter as well," Prospero replies. "But since you have given me my dukedom again, I will give you a wonder in return." He then reveals Ferdinand and Miranda, who, Prospero proclaims, are now engaged. Alonso is joyfully reunited with his son and blesses the marriage of the happy couple.

Ariel returns, driving in Caliban, Sebastian, and Trinculo, who are wet and stinking from the lake and wearing the stolen garments. Prospero reveals their plot to Alonso, who stands amazed. "Go back to your rock," Prospero tells Caliban, "and if you want to be pardoned, watch how you behave." By now, Caliban has seen the error of his ways in worshipping a drunken butler. "What a thrice-double ass was I to take this drunkard for a god, " Caliban replies, humbled. "I will be wise hereafter and seek for grace."

Satisfied with Caliban's repentance, Prospero then invites everyone into his home, where he will tell the tales of his survival. He assures them that their ship is safe and secure on another part of the island, and that it will transport them home safely. He calls to Ariel and asks the spirit to watch over their safe voyage as his last command before setting the spirit free. "Then to the elements," Prospero cries, "Be free and fare thee well!"

# CAST OF CHARACTERS

**Alonso**  King of Naples

**Sebastian**  Alonso's brother

**Prospero**  the right duke of Milan

**Antonio**  Prospero's brother, the usurping duke of Milan

**Ferdinand**  son to the king of Naples

**Gonzalo**  counselor to the king

**Adrian, Francisco**  lords from Milan

**Caliban**  a deformed slave

**Trinculo**  a jester

**Stephano**  a drunken butler

**Miranda**  daughter of Prospero

**Ariel**  an airy spirit

*Master of the ship, boatswain, and mariners*

*Other spirits attending on Prospero*

# The Tempest
## Setting

*One night, a ship tossed on the sea during a terrific storm, or tempest. Onboard were Alonso, king of Naples; his brother Sebastian; his son Ferdinand; the duke of Milan, Antonio; his faithful counselor Gonzalo; and many others. Their ship wrecked upon the waves in view of a mystical island, and all were thrown into the sea.*

## ⚜ ACT ONE ⚜

**SCENE ONE** *On a ship at sea in the middle of a terrific storm. Thunder crashes and lightning flashes in the sky.*

*Enter shipmaster and boatswain.*

**Master** Boatswain!

**Boatswain** Here master. What cheer?

**Master** Speak to the mariners. Do it soon, or we shall run ourselves aground. Hurry!

*Exit shipmaster.*

**Boatswain** Hey, you mariners! Take in the topsail; tend to the master's whistle!

*Enter Alonso, Sebastian, Antonio, Ferdinand, Gonzalo, and others.*

**Alonso** Good boatswain, have care! Where's the master?

**Boatswain** I pray now, stay below.

**Antonio** Where's the master, boatswain?

**Boatswain** Do you not hear him? You are interfering with our labors! Keep to your cabins; you do assist the storm!

**Gonzalo** Nay, good, be patient.

**Boatswain**  When the sea is. Get to your cabins! What cares the storm for the name of king? Silence! Do not trouble us now!

*Exit Sebastian, Antonio, and Alonso.*

**Gonzalo**  Yet remember who you have aboard.

**Boatswain**  None that I love more than myself. If you can command this storm to silence, we will not handle a rope more. Use your authority; if you cannot, give thanks you have lived so long, and make yourself ready in your cabin for the mischance of the hour, if it so happens. Out of our way, I say!

**Gonzalo**  I have great comfort from this fellow. Methinks he was born to be hanged!

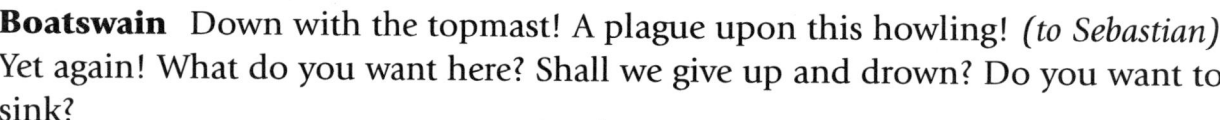

*Re-enter Sebastian and Antonio.*

**Boatswain**  Down with the topmast! A plague upon this howling! *(to Sebastian)* Yet again! What do you want here? Shall we give up and drown? Do you want to sink?

**Sebastian**  A curse on your throat, you bawling dog!

**Boatswain**  Work you, then!

**Antonio**  Hang, cur, hang! You insolent noise-maker, we are less afraid to be drowned than you are!

**Boatswain**  *(to mariners)* Hold on! Set her off to sea again!

*Enter mariner.*

**Mariner**  All is lost! To prayers, to prayers! All is lost!

**Boatswain**  Must we drown here?

**Gonzalo**  The king and prince are at prayers! Let's help them; our fate is the same.

**Sebastian**  I am out of patience.

**Antonio**  We are cheated of our lives by drunkards!

*A loud noise sounds from within.*

**Gonzalo**  Mercy on us! We split! We split! Farewell, my wife and children! Farewell, brother! We split, we split!

**Antonio**  Let's all sink with the king.

*Exit Antonio and Sebastian.*

**Gonzalo**  Now would I give a thousand miles of sea for an acre of barren ground. The wills above be done, but how I wish I could die a dry death!

**SCENE TWO**  *The island. Prospero and his daughter Miranda are watching as the ship is wrecked upon the waves.*

**Miranda**  If by your magic, my dearest father, you have put the wild waters in this roar, calm them. O! I have suffered with those who I saw suffer. A brave vessel who had no doubt some noble creatures in her, dashed all to pieces. O! The cry did knock against my very heart. Poor souls, they perished. Had I any power, I would have sunk the sea within the earth!

**Prospero**  Be calm. No more amazement. Tell your piteous heart, there's no harm done. I have done nothing but in care of thee, who is ignorant of who you are, and from where I came.

**Miranda**  I never thought to know more.

**Prospero**  'Tis time I should inform thee further. Wipe thine eyes; have comfort. The wreck that you did see I have with mine own art so safely ordered. There is no soul, nor any creature harmed in the vessel which you saw sink. Sit down, for you must now know further.

**Miranda**  You have often begun to tell me who I am, but stopped.

**Prospero**  The hour's now come. Obey, and be attentive. Can you remember a time before we came unto this island? I do not think you can, for then you were but three years old.

**Miranda**  Certainly, sir, I can. 'Tis far off and rather like a dream. Had I not four or five women once who cared for me?

**Prospero**  You did, and more, Miranda. Twelve years ago, thy father was the duke of Milan, and a prince of power. Thy mother was virtuous, and our only heir a princess.

**Miranda**  O, the heavens! What foul play brought us to this island? Or blessed was it, we did?

**Prospero**  Both, both, my girl. By foul play, as you say, were we brought; but also with divine guidance. My brother and your uncle, Antonio—oh, that a brother could be so wicked!—to him I gave the management of my state. At that time, my interests were in studying my books, and the government I gave over to my brother. My trust had no limit, and it awakened an evil nature in my brother. His ambition growing, he went to the king of Naples and promised to pay double the taxes if he would make him duke of Milan. Do you hear me?

**Miranda**  Your tale, sir, would cure deafness.

**Prospero**  This king of Naples, being an enemy, agreed to my brother's plan. So, one midnight, Antonio and his henchmen hurried us from Milan in the dead of darkness and placed us in a the rotted carcass of a boat; not rigged, nor tackle, sail, nor mast; the very rats had deserted it.

**Miranda**  Why did they not that hour destroy us?

**Prospero**  They dared not, for the people loved me dearly. So, they placed us, crying, into the sea that roared to us.

**Miranda**  How came we ashore?

**Prospero**  With divine guidance. We had some food and fresh water, which the noble Gonzalo did give us out of pity, with garments, linens, and necessaries. And of his gentleness, knowing I loved my books, he provided me from my own library, volumes that I prize above my dukedom. And here on this island we arrived; and here have I, thy schoolmaster, educated thee more than the most careful tutor.

**Miranda**  Heavens thank you for it! And now, I pray you, sir, what is your reason for raising this sea storm?

**Prospero**  By accident most strange, bountiful fortune have mine enemies brought to shore. Here cease more questions. Thou art inclined to sleep.

*He holds out his hand over Miranda. She lies down, falling asleep under the spell.*

**Prospero** Come here, Ariel! I am ready now.

*Enter Ariel.*

**Ariel** All hail, great master; hail! I come to answer thy best pleasure.

**Prospero** Hast thou, spirit, performed the tempest as I commanded?

**Ariel** To every detail. I boarded the king's ship; in every cabin I created great fear and terror. Lightning lit the sky and thunder crashed as Neptune made his bold waves tremble.

**Prospero** My brave spirit!

**Ariel** All, but mariners, fell into the foaming sea.

**Prospero** But are they safe, Ariel?

**Ariel** Not a soul perished; on their garments not a stain; and, as thou bade me, in groups have I scattered them about the island. The king's son, Ferdinand, I have landed by himself, whom I left sighing with sadness.

**Prospero** How hast thou disposed of the king's ship and all the rest of the fleet?

**Ariel** Safely in harbor is the king's ship. The mariners all under hatches stowed; whom with a charm I have left asleep. And for the rest of the fleet which I dispersed, they have all met again, and are upon the Mediterranean afloat, bound sadly home for Naples, supposing that they saw the king's ship wrecked, and his great person perish.

**Prospero** Ariel, thy charge exactly is performed. But there's more work.

**Ariel** Is there more toil? Since thou dost give me pains, let me remind thee what thou hast promised.

**Prospero** What is it thou can demand?

**Ariel** My liberty. Remember, I have done thee worthy service.

**Prospero** Dost thou forget from what torment I did free thee? Hast thou forgotten the foul witch Sycorax, who was brought here with child and left by the sailors? Thou, my slave was then her servant, and was too delicate to act her out her vile commands. With your refusal, she imprisoned thee inside a pine tree for a dozen years. Then this island (save for her son, Caliban, a freckled whelp) did not hold a human shape. Dull thing, that Caliban, whom now I keep in service. It was my magic, when I arrived, that opened the pine and let thee out.

**Ariel** I thank thee, master. I will obey thy commands, and do my spriting gently.

**Prospero** Do so, and after two days, I will free thee.

**Ariel** That's my noble master!

**Prospero** Go, make thyself like a nymph of the sea; invisible to all but me. Make thy magical music and lure the king's son to me.

*Exit Ariel.*

**Prospero** *(to Miranda)* Awake, dear heart, awake!

**Miranda** The strangeness of your story put heaviness in me.

**Prospero** Come; we'll visit Caliban, my slave, who never gives us kind answer.

**Miranda** 'Tis a villain, sir, I do not love to look on.

**Prospero** *(calling to Caliban)* Thou poisonous slave, come forth!

*Enter Caliban.*

**Caliban** This island is mine, by Sycorax my mother, which you take from me! When you came first to this island, you stroked me and made much of me. And then I loved thee, and showed thee all the qualities of the island. The fresh springs, the barren place, and the fertile. Cursed be that I did so! All the charms of Sycorax, toads, beetles, bats, come down on you! And here you imprison me in this hard rock while you keep from me the rest of the island.

**Prospero** Thou most lying slave! I have used thee, filth as thou are, with human care; and lodged thee in mine own home, till thou did seek to violate the honor of my daughter.

**Caliban** O ho! I wish it had been done! Thou did prevent me; otherwise I would have peopled this island with Calibans.

**Prospero** Wicked slave, thou art capable of only evil! I pitied thee, took pains to make thee speak, taught thee each hour one thing or other. But thy vile race could not abide good nature. Therefore you were deservedly confined into this rock.

**Caliban** You taught me language. And my profit on it is, I know how to curse. The red plague rid you for learning me your language!

**Prospero** Hag-seed, away from here! Fetch us fuel, and be quick! If you neglect what I command, I'll curse thee with cramps and aches.

**Caliban** No, prithee! *(aside)* I must obey. His magic is of great power.

*Exit Caliban. Re-enter Ariel, invisible, singing and playing music. Ferdinand is following him as if under a spell.*

**Ferdinand** Where should this music be? In the air, or the earth? As I was weeping again my father's shipwreck, this music crept by me upon the water, calming both its fury and my passion with its sweet air. Therefore, I have followed it.

**Prospero** *(to Miranda)* Say what thou seest yond.

**Miranda** *(gazing in wonder at Ferdinand)* What is it? a spirit? How it looks about! Believe me, sir, it carries a brave form. But it is a spirit.

**Prospero** No, it eats and sleeps, and has senses as we have. This gallant, which you see, was in a shipwreck; and he's stricken with grief. He has lost his fellows, and strays about to find them.

**Miranda**  I might call him a thing divine, for nothing natural I ever saw so noble.

**Prospero**  *(aside)* It goes, I see, as I planned it. *(to Ariel)* Spirit, fine spirit! I'll free thee within two days for this.

**Ferdinand**  *(seeing Miranda)* Most sure, this is the goddess for whom this music sounds! *(to Miranda)* O you wonder! Are you a human or a spirit?

**Miranda**  No wonder, sir, but certainly human.

**Prospero**  *(aside)* They have fallen in love at first sight.

**Ferdinand**  I myself am of Naples; the king's son and heir; who with mine eyes, just saw my father's ship wrecked.

**Miranda**  Alack, for mercy!

**Ferdinand**  O, maid! If your affections belong to no other, I'll make you the queen of Naples.

**Prospero**  Soft, sir; a word. *(aside)* They are both in each other's powers. But his swift business I must uneasy make, lest too light winning make the prize light. *(to Ferdinand)* Sir, a word. Thou hast put thyself upon this island as a spy, to win it from me, the lord on it.

**Ferdinand**  No, as I am a man.

**Miranda**  There's nothing ill can dwell in such a temple.

**Prospero**  *(to Ferdinand)* Follow me.—Speak not for him, daughter. He's a traitor.—Come. I'll manacle thy neck and feet together. Follow.

**Ferdinand**  No, I will resist you! *(He draws his sword, but is charmed from moving.)*

**Miranda**  O, dear father! Make not too rash a trial of him, for he's gentle, and not threatening. Sir, have pity!

**Prospero**  Silence! You think there is no more such shapes as he, having seen but him and Caliban. Foolish girl!

**Miranda**  I have no ambition to see a goodlier man.

**Prospero**  Come on—obey.

*Ferdinand is slowly regaining the strength in his arms and legs.*

**Ferdinand**  My senses, as in a dream, are all bound up. My father's loss, the weakness which I feel, the wreck of all my friends, nor this man's threats, to whom I am subdued, are but light to me, might I but through my prison once a day behold this maid.

**Prospero**  *(aside)* It works!—Come on.—Thou hast done well, fine Ariel!

# ACT TWO

**SCENE ONE**  *Another part of the island.*

*Enter Alonso, Sebastian, Antonio, Gonzalo, Adrian, Francisco, and others.*

**Gonzalo**  Please you, sir, be merry. We all have cause of joy, for our escape is much beyond our loss. Weigh our sorrow with our comfort.

**Alonso**  Prithee, peace.

**Sebastian**  He receives comfort like cold porridge.

**Adrian**  The air breathes upon us here most sweetly.

**Sebastian**  As if it had rotten lungs.

**Antonio**  *(mocking, rolling his eyes)* Or as it were perfumed by a swamp.

**Gonzalo**  Here everything is advantageous to life.

**Antonio**  True; save means to live.

**Sebastian**  Of that, there's none or little.

**Gonzalo**  How lush the grass looks! How green!

**Antonio**  The ground, indeed, is quite tawny.

**Gonzalo**  Methinks our garments are now as fresh as when we put them on in Africa at the marriage of the king's fair daughter Claribel to the king of Tunis.

**Sebastian**  *(sarcastically)* 'Twas a sweet marriage, and we prosper well in our return.

**Alonso**  You cram these words into mine ears when I would rather forget. I wish I had never married my daughter there! For, coming back, my son is lost; and she too, who is so far from Italy now. I never shall see her again. O my son! What strange fish has made his meal on thee?

**Francisco**  Sir, he may live. I saw him ride upon the waves, beating them back. I doubt not, he came alive to land.

**Alonso**  No, no; he's gone.

**Sebastian**  Sir, you may thank yourself for this loss. You would not bless Europe with your daughter, but rather lose her to Africa; where she is lost to you.

**Alonso**  Prithee, peace.

**Sebastian**  We have lost your son, I fear, forever. The fault is your own.

**Gonzalo**  My Lord Sebastian, the truth you speak lacks some gentleness. You rub the sore, when you should bring a remedy.

**Sebastian**  Very well.

**Gonzalo**  If I governed here on this island, I would admit no trade, no magistrate, no riches or poverty, no occupation—all men would be idle, and all women, too, but innocent and pure; and no monarchy . . .

**Sebastian**  Yet he would be king on it.

**Gonzalo**  All things in nature should produce, without work or sweat. Treason, felony, sword, knife, gun, I would not have; but nature should bring forth, of its own kind, all abundance to feed my innocent people.

**Sebastian**  Save his majesty!

**Antonio**  Long live Gonzalo!

*Enter Ariel, invisible, with solemn music playing. All the men fall asleep under his spell except Alonso, Sebastian, and Antonio.*

**Alonso**  What! All so soon asleep? I wish mine eyes would shut off my thoughts. *(He begins to feel sleepy.)* I find they are inclined to do so.

**Antonio**  We two, my lord, will guard your person while you take your rest, and watch your safety.

**Alonso**  Thank you. Wondrous heavy . . . *(He falls asleep.)*

*Exit Ariel.*

**Sebastian**  What a strange drowsiness possesses them!

**Antonio**  It is the quality of the climate.

**Sebastian**  I do not find myself inclined to sleep.

**Antonio**  Nor I. My spirits are lively. They all fell asleep together, as if by command.—Sebastian, methinks, I see it in thy face, what thou should be. My strong imagination sees a crown dropping upon thy head.

**Sebastian**  What! Art thou waking?

**Antonio**  Noble Sebastian, you are allowing your fortune to sleep, die rather, while you are waking. Do you agree that Ferdinand is drowned?

**Sebastian**  He's gone.

**Antonio**  Then tell me, who's the next heir of Naples?

**Sebastian**  Claribel.

**Antonio**  She who is Queen of Tunis; she who dwells so far from Naples that she hears no news. Because of this Claribel we were sea-swallowed, though some survived; and by that destiny to perform an act, whereof what's past is prologue, and what to come is in our hands.

**Sebastian**  What stuff is this! How say you? 'Tis true, my brother's daughter is queen of Tunis; so is she heir of Naples; between which regions there is some space.

**Antonio**  A space whose every cubit seems to cry out, "How shall that Claribel come back to Naples? Stay in Tunis, and let Sebastian wake!" There be that can rule Naples as well as he that sleeps. O, that you had the mind that I do! Do you understand me?

**Sebastian**  Methinks I do.

**Antonio**  And what do you think of this good fortune?

**Sebastian**  I remember, you did overthrow your brother Prospero.

**Antonio** True. And look how well my garments sit upon me; much better than before. My brother's servants were then my fellows, now they are my men.

**Sebastian** Thy case, dear friend, shall be my example. As thou took Milan, I'll take Naples. Draw thy sword. One stroke shall free thee from the tribute which thou pay'st, and I the king shall love thee.

**Antonio** Draw together; and when I raise my hand, do you the like, to kill Gonzalo.

**Sebastian** But one word. *(They move close together and whisper.)*

*Re-enter Ariel, invisible.*

**Ariel** Through his magic, my master foresees the danger that you, his friends, are in; and sends me forth to keep you living. *(He sings in Gonzalo's ear.)* "While you here do snoring lie, open-eyed conspiracy his time doth take. If of life you keep a care, shake off sleep, and beware. Awake!"

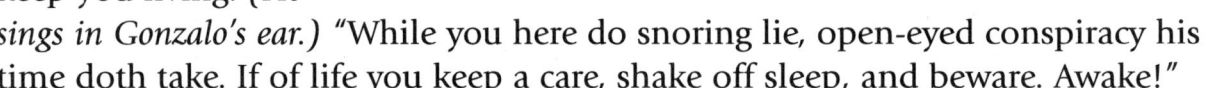

**Antonio** Then let us both be sudden.

*As Antonio and Sebastian approach the king and Gonzalo with their swords raised to strike, everyone wakes up.*

**Alonso** Why, how now! Awake! Why are you drawn?

**Gonzalo** What's the matter?

**Sebastian** While we stood here securing your slumber, even now, we heard a hollow burst of bellowing like bulls, or rather lions. Did it not wake you?

**Alonso** I heard nothing. Heard you this, Gonzalo?

**Gonzalo** Upon mine honor, sir, I heard a humming which did wake me. 'Tis best we stand on our guard, or that we leave this place, Let's draw our weapons.

**Alonso** Lead us off this ground, and let's search further for my poor son.

*Exit all but Ariel.*

**Ariel** Prospero shall know what I have done. So, king, safely on to find thy son.

**SCENE TWO** *Another part of the island.*

*Enter Caliban with a burden of wood. Thunder crashes overhead.*

**Caliban** All the infections that the sun sucks up from bogs and swamps, on Prospero fall, and give him a disease! Lo, now, lo! Here comes a spirit of his to torment me for bringing wood in slowly. I'll fall flat; perchance, he will not mind me.

*Caliban falls to the ground. Enter Trinculo.*

**Trinculo** Here's neither bush nor shrub to bear off any weather at all, and another storm forming. *(He sees Caliban lying on the ground.)* What have we here? A man or a fish? Dead or alive? A fish! He smells like a fish! Legged like a man, and his fins like arms! This is no fish, but an islander that has lately suffered a lightning bolt. *(Thunder crashes.)* Alas! The storm is come again. My best way is to creep under his cloak; there is no other shelter hereabout. Misery acquaints a man with strange bedfellows. I will hide here till the storm passes.

*Trinculo lies next to Caliban and pulls Caliban's cloak over both of them, covering everything but their feet. Enter Stephano with a bottle of wine.*

**Stephano** Well, here's my comfort. *(He drinks and stumbles.)*

**Caliban** Do not torment me!

**Stephano** What's the matter? Have we monsters here? Ha! I have not escaped drowning to be afraid now of your four legs.

**Caliban** The spirit torments me!

**Stephano** This is some four-legged monster of the island who has a fever.

**Caliban** Do not torment me, prithee! I'll bring my wood home faster.

**Stephano** He's in his fit now, and does not make sense. He shall taste of my bottle. If he has never drunk wine before, it will remove his fit.

*He pours wine into Caliban's mouth.*

**Trinculo** I should know that voice. It should be—but he is drowned, and these are monsters. O! Defend me!

**Stephano** Four legs and two voices! A most delicate monster!

**Trinculo** Stephano!

**Stephano** Does thy other mouth call me? Mercy! Mercy!

**Trinculo** Stephano! If thou be Stephano, speak to me, for I am Trinculo. Be not afraid; I am thy good friend Trinculo.

*Trinculo sits up, removing the cloak.*

**Stephano** Thou art Trinculo indeed! How came you to be with this monster?

**Trinculo** I took him to be killed with a lightning bolt. But art thou not drowned, Stephano? O Stephano! We two have escaped!

**Caliban** These be fine things if they are not sprites. That's a brave god, and bears celestial liquor. I will kneel to him.

*Caliban falls to his knees in front of Stephano.*

**Stephano** How now, monster? How is thy fever?

**Caliban** Hast thou not dropped from heaven? I adore thee!

**Stephano** Come, swear to that; take a drink.

*Stephano holds out the bottle to Caliban, and Caliban drinks from it.*

**Caliban** I'll show thee every fertile inch of the island, and I will kiss thy foot. I prithee, be my god!

**Trinculo**  By this light, a most evil and drunken monster.

**Caliban**  I'll kiss thy foot. I'll swear myself thy servant. I'll show thee the best springs; I'll pluck thee berries; I'll fish for thee, and get thee wood. A plague upon the tyrant who I serve! I'll follow thee, thou wondrous man!

**Trinculo**  A most ridiculous monster to make a wonder of a poor drunkard!

**Stephano**  I prithee now, lead the way without any more talking. Trinculo, the king and all our company being drowned, we will inherit here.

**Caliban**  *(singing drunkenly)* Farewell, master; farewell, farewell! No more dams I'll make for fish, nor scrape his plate, nor wash his dish. 'Ban, 'Ban, Ca-Caliban, has a new master—got a new man! *(He shouts excitedly, dancing about.)* Freedom, freedom! Hey-day! Hey-day! Freedom, freedom!

**Trinculo**  A howling drunken monster!

**Stephano**  Brave monster, lead the way!

## ⚜ ACT THREE ⚜

**SCENE ONE** *In the woods near Prospero's home.*

*Enter Ferdinand carrying a log.*

**Ferdinand**  Some sports are painful, but their labor is worth the pleasure they give. This base task would be burdensome to me, but the mistress I serve makes my labors pleasures. O, she is ten times more gentle than her father, for he's made of only harshness. I must remove some thousands of these logs and pile them up. My sweet mistress weeps when she sees me work; and says, such baseness had never been done by one so honorable. These sweet thoughts do refresh my labors.

*Enter Miranda; and Prospero at a distance, watching.*

**Miranda**  Pray you, work not so hard. I wish that lightning had burnt up those logs you must pile. My father is hard at study, so rest yourself. He's safe for these three hours.

**Ferdinand**  Dear mistress! The sun will set before I finish what I strive to do.

**Miranda**  If you'll sit down, I'll bear your logs the while. *(She reaches for the log he is carrying.)* Pray, give me that. I'll carry it to the pile.

**Ferdinand**  No, precious creature. I had rather crack my sinews, break my back, than you should undergo such dishonor while I sit lazy by.

**Prospero**  *(aside)* Poor worm! Thou art infected. This clearly shows it.

**Miranda**  You look weary.

**Ferdinand**  No, noble mistress; it is fresh morning with me when you are by at night. I beg you, what is your name?

**Miranda**  Miranda. *(She gasps and clasps her hand over her mouth.)* O father! I have broken your rules to say so.

**Ferdinand**  Admired Miranda! Indeed, the top of admiration; worth what's dearest to the world!

**Miranda**  I do not know one of my sex; no woman's face do I remember except my own in the mirror; nor have I any I may call men other than thou, good friend, and my dear father. But, by my modesty, I would not wish any companion in the world but you.

**Ferdinand**  I am a prince, Miranda; I do think, a king; and would no more suffer this wooden slavery than a blow to the mouth. Hear my soul speak—the very instant that I saw you, my heart flew to your service, and I am slave to it. And for your sake, I am this patient log-man.

**Miranda**  Do you love me?

**Ferdinand**  I, more than the world, do love, prize, and honor you.

**Miranda**  Then I am your wife, if you will marry me; if not, I'll die your maid.

**Ferdinand**  My mistress, dearest, and I thus humble ever.

**Miranda**  My husband then?

**Ferdinand**  Ay, with all my heart. Here's my hand. *(He takes her hand.)*

**Miranda**  And mine, with my heart in it. And now, farewell.

*Exit Ferdinand and Miranda, going separate ways.*

**Prospero**  I am glad of this, and rejoice. But I'll back to my books; for yet, before suppertime, I must perform much important business.

---
**SCENE TWO**  *Another part of the island.*

---

*Enter Caliban with a bottle; Stephano and Trinculo following.*

**Stephano**  My man-monster has drowned his tongue in wine. *(to Caliban)* Speak if thou art a good monster.

**Caliban**  How does thy honor? Let me lick thy shoe. *(pointing to Trinculo)* I'll not serve him; he is not valiant.

**Trinculo**  Most ignorant monster. Thou deboshed fish thou, was ever a man a coward who has drunk so much wine as I today? Will thou tell a monstrous lie, being but half a fish, and half a monster?

**Caliban**  Lo, how he mocks me!—Will thou let him, my lord?

**Stephano**  Trinculo, keep a good tongue in your head. If you prove to be a mutineer, I'll hang you from the next tree! The poor monster's my subject, and he shall not suffer abuse.

**Caliban**  I thank my lord. Will thou listen once again to the plot I told thee?

*Enter Ariel, invisible.*

**Caliban**  As I told thee before, I am subject to a tyrant; a sorcerer, that by his cunning has cheated me of this island.

**Ariel**  *(imitating Trinculo)* Thou liest!

**Caliban**  *(to Trinculo)* Thou liest, thou joking monkey! I wish my valiant master would destroy thee. I do not lie!

**Stephano**  Trinculo, if you trouble him more, I will knock out some of your teeth.

**Trinculo**  I said nothing.

**Stephano**  Then proceed, monster.

**Caliban**  I say, by sorcery he got this island from me. If thy greatness will revenge it on him, thou shalt be lord of it, and I'll serve thee.

**Stephano**  How shall this be accomplished? Can thou bring me to the sorcerer?

**Caliban**  Yea, yea, my lord. I'll yield him to thee as he sleeps, where thou may knock a nail into his head. 'Tis habit with him to sleep in the afternoon. There thou may brain him, having first seized his books. For without them, he's but a sot, and has not one spirit to command. And another thing to consider is the beauty of his daughter.

**Stephano**  Is she so brave a lass?

**Caliban**  Ay, lord. She will become thy wife, and bring thee forth brave brood.

**Stephano**  Monster, I will kill this man. His daughter and I will be king and queen. Trinculo and thyself shall be viceroys. Dost thou like the plot, Trinculo?

**Trinculo**  Excellent!

**Ariel**  This will I tell my master!

**Caliban**  Thou makest me merry. I am full of pleasure; let us be jocund!

**Stephano**  Lead, monster. We'll follow.

**SCENE THREE**  *Another part of the island.*

*Enter Alonso, Sebastian, Antonio, Gonzalo, Adrian, Francisco, and others.*

**Gonzalo**  I can go no further, sir; my old bones ache. Please, I need to rest.

**Alonso**  Old lord, I cannot blame thee; I myself am weary. Sit down and rest. Here I will give up hope. My son, for whom we search, must be drowned.

**Antonio**  *(aside to Sebastian)* I am right glad that he's so out of hope. Do not, for one moment, forget our purpose.

**Sebastian**  *(aside to Antonio)* Let it be tonight, for now they are weary with travel.

*Solemn and strange music sounds, and Prospero enters and stands in the background. He is invisible to the others. Enter several strange spirits, bringing in a banquet. They dance about the table and invite the king and all the others to eat. The spirits then vanish.*

**Alonso**  What harmony is this? My good friends, listen!

**Gonzalo**  These are monstrous shapes, yet their manners are quite gentle.

**Prospero**  *(aside)* Honest lord, thou hast said well; for some of you are devils.

**Francisco**  They vanished strangely.

**Sebastian**  No matter, since they have left their banquet behind, for we are hungry.—Will it please you to taste of what is here?

**Alonso**  I will go and feed, although my last. No matter, since I feel the best is past. Brother, my lord, the duke, do as we do.

*Thunder crashes and lightning lights up the sky. Enter Ariel like a harpy. He spreads his great wings over the table, and the banquet vanishes.*

**Ariel**  *(to Alonso, Sebastian, and Antonio)* You are three sinful men whom destiny has caused the sea to belch upon island, where man doth not inhabit; you amongst men being most unfit to live! I have made you mad. *(Alonso, Sebastian, and Antonio draw their swords.)* You fools! I and my fellows are ministers of fate. Your swords are now too heavy for your strengths, and will not be uplifted. But remember, that you three from Milan did supplant good Prospero, and exposed him and his innocent child unto the sea. For which foul deed the powers have incensed the seas and shores, yea, all the creatures, against your peace!

*Ariel vanishes. Then, to soft music, the shapes enter again and carry out the table.*

**Prospero** (*aside*) Bravely the figure of this harpy hast thou performed, my Ariel. My instruction you have clearly followed, and with grace. My high charms work; and these, mine enemies, are all bound up in their confusion. They now are in my power; and in these fits I leave them while I visit young Ferdinand (whom they supposed drowned) and my darling daughter.

*Exit Prospero.*

**Gonzalo** Sir, why stand you here staring so strangely?

**Alonso** O, it is monstrous! Methought the waves spoke and told me of my sins; therefore, my son is bedded in mud; and there I will seek him, and lie with him.

*Exit Alonso.*

**Sebastian** But one fiend at a time! I'll fight armies of them.

**Antonio** I'll be thy second.

*Exit Sebastian and Antonio.*

**Gonzalo** All three of them are desperate. Their great guilt, like slow-working poison, now begins to bite them. Adrian, I do beseech you, follow them and prevent them from what they may feel provoked to do.

##  ACT FOUR

**SCENE ONE** *Before Prospero's home.*

*Enter Prospero, Ferdinand, and Miranda.*

**Prospero** If I have too harshly punished you, your marriage to my daughter makes amends; for I have given you here a thread of mine own life, or that for which I live; whom once again I tender to thy hand. All thy vexations were but my trials of thy love, and you have stood the test. Here, before heaven, I give thee my rich gift. Take my daughter. Now, sit and talk with her; she is thine own.—Ariel, my industrious servant Ariel!

*Enter Ariel.*

**Ariel** What may I do for you, master? Here I am.

**Prospero** You performed your last service most worthily, and I must use you in such another trick. Go, bring the rabble over whom I give thee power, here, to this place. Place upon the eyes of this young couple some of my magic. It is my promise, and they expect it from me. Now come, my Ariel. Bring before us many spirits to perform for our pleasure. No tongue, all eyes; be silent.

*Soft music sounds as many beautiful spirits appear in the forms of Iris, goddess of the rainbow; Ceres, goddess of the harvest; and Juno, queen of the gods and goddesses. They are elaborately costumed, and they perform dances in celebration of Ferdinand's and Miranda's engagement.*

**Ferdinand** This is a most majestic vision, most harmonious and charming! May I be bold to think these are spirits?

**Prospero** Spirits, which by my magic I have called, to act out my present fancies.

**Ferdinand** Let me live here forever! So rare a wondered father, and a wife, makes this place paradise.

*Enter more spirits, who join the nymphs in a graceful dance. Toward the end of the dance, Prospero appears distracted, and then speaks suddenly. The dancers, confused, vanish at the sudden sound.*

**Prospero** *(aside)* I had forgot that foul conspiracy of the beast Caliban and his conspirators against my life. The minute of their plot is almost come.

**Ferdinand** This is strange. Your father's in a passion that works him strongly.

**Miranda** Never till this day have I seen him touched with anger so distempered.

**Prospero** *(to Ferdinand)* My son, you look worried. Be cheerful. Our revels now are ended. These our actors, as I foretold you, were all spirits, and are melted into thin air. We are such stuff as dreams are made on, and our little life is rounded with a sleep. But sir, I am vexed. Bear with my weakness; my old brain is troubled. Be not disturbed with my infirmity. If you be pleased, retire into my home, and there repose. I'll take a walk to still my troubled mind.

**Ferdinand, Miranda** We wish your peace.

**Prospero** I thank thee.

*Exit Ferdinand and Miranda.*

**Prospero** Ariel, come!

*Enter Ariel.*

**Ariel** What's thy pleasure, good master?

**Prospero** We must prepare to meet with Caliban. Where did thou leave these varlets?

**Ariel** So full of valor that they curse the air for breathing in their faces, yet always bending towards their project. I beat my drum to charm their ears, and they, calf-like, followed. At last I left them in the filthy pool beyond your home, there dancing up to their chins, the foul lake overstinking their feet.

**Prospero** This was well done, my bird. Retain thy invisible shape. Bring me some clothing and trinkets from my house as bait to catch these thieves.

**Ariel** I go, I go.

*Exit Ariel.*

**Prospero** That Caliban is a born monster, on whose nature nurture can never stick; on whom my teachings are quite lost. And as with age his body grows uglier. I will plague them all!

*Re-enter Ariel, carrying colorful clothing and trinkets.*

**Prospero**  Come, hang them on this line.

*Enter Caliban, Stephano, and Trinculo, wet and stinking from the lake.*

**Caliban**  Pray you, walk softly, that the blind mole may not hear a foot fall; we are near his home. This is the place. Do that good mischief, which may make this island thine own forever, and I thy Caliban, thy foot-licker.

**Stephano**  Give me thy hand. I do begin to have bloody thoughts.

**Trinculo**  O worthy King Stephano! Look what a wardrobe is here for thee!

**Caliban**  Do not dote on such luggage! Leave it alone, and do the murder first.

**Stephano**  Be quiet, monster. Help carry this away to where my barrel of wine is, or I'll turn you out of my kingdom. Go to; carry this.

*Enter several spirits disguised as hounds. They chase Stephano, Trinculo, and Caliban away as Prospero and Ariel urge them on.*

**Prospero**  Ariel, command my goblins to infect their joints with painful cramps and convulsions! Let them be hunted soundly. At this hour all mine enemies lie at my mercy. Shortly shall all my labors end, and thou shalt have your freedom. For a while longer, follow and do me service.

# ACT FIVE

**SCENE ONE** *Before the home of Prospero.*

*Enter Prospero in his magic robes, and Ariel.*

**Prospero**  Now my plot nears its end. Say, my spirit, how fares the king and his followers?

**Ariel**  Confined together in the same fashion as you ordered; just as you left them. All prisoners, sir, in the lime grove. They cannot budge till your release. The king, his brother, and yours, are all three distracted, and the remainder mourning over them, full of sorrow. Your magic so strongly works on them, that if you now saw them, your affections would become tender.

**Prospero**  Dost thou think so, spirit?

**Ariel**  Mine would, sir, were I human.

**Prospero**  And mine shall. With their evil deeds I am deeply offended, yet my nobler reason controls my fury. It is better to forgive than to take revenge. If they are penitent, my purpose is fulfilled. Go release them, Ariel. My charms I'll break, their senses I'll restore, and they shall be themselves.

**Ariel**  I'll fetch them, sir.

*Exit Ariel.*

**Prospero**  But this rough magic I here give up; and, when I have worked some magic upon their senses, I'll break my staff, bury it in the earth, and drown my books in the sea.

*Solemn music sounds. Re-enter Ariel with Alonso, Sebastian, and Antonio, who appear spellbound; Gonzalo, Francisco, and Adrian follow. They form a circle which Prospero has made, and there stand charmed.*

40 The Tempest                                            ©1998 Good Apple

**Prospero** There stand, for you are spell-stopped. *(to Gonzalo)* O good Gonzalo! My true preserver and honorable sir. I will repay your loyalties, both in word and deed. *(to Alonso)* Most cruelly didst thou, Alonso, use me and my daughter. Thy brother was an accomplice to the act. *(to Sebastian)* Thou art feeling guilty for it now, Sebastian. *(to Antonio)* My flesh and blood, my brother, whose ambition replaced your good nature, who, with Sebastian here would have killed your king. I do forgive thee, unnatural though thou art. *(aside)* Their reason begins to return; soon their understanding will be clear.

*Re-enter Ariel, singing and helping Prospero put on his magical robes.*

**Prospero** My Ariel! I shall miss thee. But thou shall have thy freedom. Go to the king's ship, invisible as thou art. There you shall find the mariners asleep. Awaken them and bring them to this place.

*Exit Ariel. The men are slowly regaining feeling and movement in their limbs as if they are awakening from a dream.*

**Gonzalo** All torment, trouble, wonder, and amazement inhabits here. Some heavenly power guide us out of this fearful country!

**Prospero** Behold, sir king, the wronged duke of Milan, Prospero. For more assurance that a living prince does now speak to thee, I embrace thy body; and to thee, and thy company, I bid a hearty welcome. *(Prospero embraces Alonso.)*

**Alonso** Since I saw thee, the madness of my mind amends. If you are truly Prospero, this makes a most strange story. Thy dukedom I resign; and do beg thou pardon me my wrongs.—But how should Prospero be living and be here?

**Prospero** You do yet taste some magic of this island that will not let you believe things certain.—Welcome, my friends all.—*(aside to Sebastian and Antonio)* But you, my evil lords, were I so minded, I could expose you and show you as traitors. At this time I will tell no tales.

**Sebastian** *(aside)* The devil speaks in him.

**Prospero** No. *(to Antonio)* As for you, most wicked sir, whom to call brother would infect my mouth, I do forgive thy rankest fault; and require my dukedom of thee, which I know thou must restore.

**Alonso** If thou art Prospero, give us details of your survival: How thou met us here, who three hours since were wrecked upon this shore; where I have lost my dear son Ferdinand.

**Prospero**  I am woe for it, sir.

**Alonso**  The loss is irreparable.

**Prospero**  As great to me, as late, for I have lost my daughter.

**Alonso**  A daughter? O heavens! That they were living both in Naples, the king and queen there! When did you lose your daughter?

**Prospero**  In this last tempest. But pray you, sir, look inside my home. Since you have given me my dukedom again, I will give you a wonder in return; at least, to content you as my dukedom pleases me.

*The entrance to the Prospero's home opens, revealing Ferdinand and Miranda, who are playing chess.*

**Alonso**  If this prove a vision of the island, one dear son shall I twice lose.

**Sebastian**  A most high miracle!

*Ferdinand approaches his father and drops to his knees before him.*

**Ferdinand**  Though the seas threaten, they are merciful. I have cursed them without cause!

**Alonso**  Now all the blessings of a glad father surround thee!

**Miranda**  O wonder! How many goodly creatures are there here! How beauteous mankind is! O brave new world, that has such people in it!

**Prospero**  'Tis new to thee.

**Alonso**  Who is this maid, with whom thou was at play?

**Ferdinand**  By gracious fate, she is mine. I chose her, when I could not ask my father for his advice, nor thought I had one. She is daughter to this famous duke of Milan, of whom so often I have heard renown, but never saw before; of whom I have received a second life; and second father this lady makes him to me.

**Alonso** *(to Ferdinand and Miranda)* Give me your hands. Let grief and sorrow embrace the heart that does not wish you joy!

*Re-enter Ariel with the captain and boatswain, who follow in amazement.*

**Gonzalo** O look, sir! Here is more of us. What is the news?

**Boatswain** Our ship is tight, and secure, and bravely rigged, as when we first put out to sea.

**Ariel** *(aside to Prospero)* Sir, all this service have I done since I went.

**Prospero** *(aside to Ariel)* My tricksy spirit!

**Boatswain** We were dead of sleep under the hatches, and then horrible sounds awakened us. We observed our gallant ship, and then were brought hither, confused and amazed.

**Ariel** *(aside to Prospero)* Was it well done?

**Prospero** *(aside to Ariel)* Bravely, my spirit! Thou shall be free. But now, set Caliban and his companions free; untie the spell.

*Exit Ariel.*

**Prospero** *(to Alonso)* How fares my gracious sir? There are yet missing of your company some few odd lads that you remember not.

*Re-enter Ariel driving in Caliban, Stephano, and Trinculo in their stolen clothing.*

**Prospero** Mark the clothing of these men, my lords, then say if they be honest. These three have robbed me; and this demi-monster had plotted with them to take my life. Two of these fellows you must know, and own; this thing of darkness I acknowledge as mine.

**Caliban** I shall be pinched to death!

**Sebastian** Why, how now, Stephano?

**Stephano** *(moaning in pain)* O, touch me not! I am not Stephano, but a horrible, painful cramp!

**Prospero** You were going to be king of the island, were you?

**Stephano** I should have been a sore one then.

**Alonso** *(pointing to Caliban)* This is a strange thing as ever I looked on.

**Prospero** He is as deformed in his manners as in his shape. *(to Caliban)* Go, sirrah, to my cell; take with you your companions. As you look to have my pardon, mind how you behave.

**Caliban** Ay, that I will; and I'll be wise hereafter, and seek for grace. What a thrice-double ass was I, to take this drunkard for a god, and worship this dull fool!

**Prospero** Go to; away!

*Exit Caliban, Stephano, and Trinculo.*

**Prospero** Sir, I invite your highness and your followers to my poor home, where you shall take your rest for this one night. And in the morning, I'll bring you to your ship, and so to Naples, where I have hope to see the marriage of our dear-beloved children. And then retire me to my Milan.

**Alonso** I long to hear the story of your life, which must take the ear strangely.

**Prospero** I'll deliver all; and promise you calm seas and journey so speedy that you shall catch your royal fleet. *(to Ariel)* My Ariel! Those are my commands; then to the elements! Be free, and fare thee well!

# VOCABULARY

## ACT ONE

**abide** accept
**alack** expression of sorrow
**ambition** strong desire to achieve
**bade** commanded
**barren** producing little vegetation
**boatswain** officer on a ship
**bountiful** plentiful
**brave** splendid; excellent
**carcass** frame; structure
**charge** command
**confined** imprisoned
**cur** coward
**divine** holy
**fertile** productive; healthy
**gallant** fine gentleman
**goodlier** better
**hag-seed** child of a witch
**hatches** openings in a ship's deck
**heir** one who inherits property
**henchmen** criminal gang members
**ignorant** unknowing; innocent
**insolent** insulting
**manacle** chain
**Neptune** Roman god of the sea
**nymph** female spirit
**perished** died violently
**piteous** compassionate
**plague** fatal disease
**rash** harsh and quick
**rigged** fitted with sails
**spriting** acts of a fairy or spirit
**stowed** stored
**subdued** enslaved to punishment
**tackle** system of ropes on a ship
**tempest** wild storm
**toil** hard work
**vile** gross; disgusting
**violate** attack
**virtuous** moral and good
**whelp** young, rude fellow
**yond** over there

## ACT TWO

**abundance** plenty
**acquaints** familiarizes
**advantageous** favorable
**bellowing** roaring
**bogs** marshes
**celestial** heavenly; of gods or angels
**conspiracy** agreement to perform an evil or illegal act
**cubit** measure of length
**felony** serious crime
**idle** unemployed; inactive
**inclined** tendency for
**infections** diseases
**lush** luxurious; full
**magistrate** officers with the power to enforce laws
**mocking** making fun of
**monarchy** government by one king
**poverty** being poor
**prologue** introductory event
**prosper** succeed
**sarcastic** mocking; taunting
**tawny** golden brown
**torment** torture; cause pain
**treason** betrayal of one's own country
**tribute** money paid from one country to another for protection
**tyrant** cruel ruler

# VOCABULARY

## ACT THREE

**base** low; uneducated

**bear** carry

**brain** hit on the head

**brood** children

**burdensome** difficult to bear

**cunning** trickery

**deboshed** corrupt; evil

**exposed** placed in danger's way

**fiend** wicked person

**harpy** monster with a woman's head and a bird's wings, tail, and claws

**humble** submissive; not proud

**incensed** angered

**jocund** joyous; merry

**mutineer** one who rebels against a superior

**proceed** go forward

**sinews** muscular strength

**solemn** gloomy; serious

**sorcerer** magician

**sot** stupid fool

**strive** work hard toward a goal

**supplant** take the place of

**valiant** courageous; brave

**viceroys** governors

## ACT FOUR

**amends** makes up for insult or injury

**convulsions** seizures

**distempered** disturbed

**dote** show excessive attention or affection

**fancies** images of the mind

**foretold** told beforehand

**industrious** hard-working; skillful

**infect** give a disease to

**infirmity** sickness

**majestic** wonderfully grand

**nature** a person's character

**nurture** influence of environment on a person

**rabble** mob of people

**repose** lie at rest

**retain** keep

**retire** go in for rest

**revels** festivities

**rounded** made complete

**trinkets** small objects of little value

**valor** courage; boldness

**varlets** rascals; rude fellows

**vexations** sources of annoyance

## ACT FIVE

**accomplice** partner in crime

**demi-monster** one-half monster, one-half human

**distracted** confused; bewildered

**dull** stupid

**elements** powers of the air and heavens

**fares** gets along

**hearty** whole-hearted

**irreparable** cannot be fixed

**mark** pay attention to

**offended** sinned against

**penitent** sorry for past sins

**preserver** rescuer

**rankest** most evil

**renown** widely honored; famed

**resign** give up an office

**thrice** three times

**woe** sorrowful

# INTRODUCING DRAMA

 "All the world's a stage, and all the men and women merely players." This quote from Shakespeare's delightful comedy *As You Like It* is a great way to begin your study of Shakespeare. Ask students what they think this quote means. Explain that "players" are actually "actors." Shakespeare meant that throughout our lives, we play many different roles—children, teenagers, and adults; daughters, sons, mothers, fathers, cousins, friends, workers, and so on. We also "act" within our life roles. Play-acting is a part of everyday existence. Ask students when they might "act" in real life. Invite them to act out an incident from their lives for the class (for example, a problem with a sibling, a funny incident with a family member or friend, or an embarrassing moment). Students can have lots of fun with this; encourage them to be creative, yet true to life.

 Ask students if they have ever seen a stage play. Discuss the difference between acting onstage, in the movies, or on TV. In Shakespeare's time, there were no TVs, movies, radios, or video games, so entertainment usually came in the form of drama. Drama did not begin with Shakespeare. Plays were watched with rapt attention by theatregoers many centuries before him. Drama is thought to have developed from many sources—an outgrowth of religious ceremonies to appease the gods; songs at grave sites or about heroes, extolling their virtues; to preach morals to the masses; and simply to satisfy people's natural love for storytelling and entertainment. Drama was and still is a way to "get away from it all" and have a good time. It creates an opportunity for us to laugh at ourselves as we see life reflected in the many human characters and situations portrayed before us.

Showing videotapes of Shakespearean plays helps children understand the nuances of drama, and how Shakespeare's language and characterizations bring his stories to life. Many of Shakespeare's plays are available on videotape. Watch a video and/or compare one video interpretation to another. Make sure to view videos before showing them to your class, as some material may be unsuitable due to language or adult situations. However, don't let videos replace the reading and performing of plays by your students. Shakespeare is meant to be experienced as a live performance.

# THE LANGUAGE OF SHAKESPEARE

At first, "Shakespearean language" can seem overwhelming to students. Many students have heard Shakespeare quoted, but have no idea what these quotes mean. Though the language may seem complex, it was common in England at the time the plays were written. It's no wonder students may feel overwhelmed reading even an edited version of a Shakespearean play. It's been estimated that he uses between 25,000 and 29,000 different words in his plays and poems! But among all the "thees" and "thous" are many common, everyday expressions students will be amazed to know originated with Shakespeare (or "the bard"). Write several of these Shakespearean expressions on the board and invite students to guess what they mean. They'll be surprised at how these expressions have endured through time.

- Apple of her eye
- Bated breath
- Budge an inch
- Dead as a door nail
- Eating me out of house and home
- Eyesore
- For goodness' sake
- The game is up
- Good riddance
- Green-eyed monster
- Household words
- Knock, knock, who's there?
- Laughingstock
- The naked truth
- Neither rhyme nor reason
- One fell swoop
- The primrose path
- Such stuff as dreams are made on
- Suit the action to the word
- Sweets to the sweet
- To thine own self be true
- Too much of a good thing
- Tower of strength
- Wear my heart on my sleeve
- What's done is done

# LET'S PUT ON A PLAY!

If you decide to produce the play, you can make it as small or as large a production as you like. You may decide on just an "in-class" production, maybe inviting one or two classes to the performance; or you may want to perform for parents or the whole school. Decide which experience would most benefit your students and meet your classroom needs. When deciding the kind of production you want, consider the time you will need to invest and your classroom budget. It's advantageous for students to be able to perform more than once so they can evaluate and discuss areas for improvement.

Discuss with students which type of production they prefer. Do they want a "classic" Shakespearean production, or do they want to get creative with their interpretation? Students can modernize the play, set it in a different time and/or place, or they can interject their own vernacular. There are many innovative ways to approach a Shakespearean production, so encourage students to brainstorm how they can make theirs original and interesting. Remind them that the fun of putting on a play is in the *process*, not necessarily the *performance*. Make it simple (props, costumes, scenery) so students will get the most out of the experience.

*When deciding the kind of production you want, consider the time you will need to invest and your classroom budget.*

Most students will want to act in the play, and there's a good chance that several will want the leading roles. Since one purpose of performing plays is to increase self-esteem and self-confidence, it wouldn't make sense to choose only the most poised, confident students in the class. On the other hand, choosing a cast of shy, introverted actors will lessen the strength of and interest in the play. If possible, try and balance your cast. It's also helpful to choose actors who will help each other develop their parts in the friendly spirit of cooperation. Since there are fewer female than male roles, allow girls to play boys' parts and vice versa. Consider the following questions when choosing actors.

- **Does the student have a voice that carries? If not, can he or she bring up the voice level?**

- **Does the student show imagination and enthusiasm for the part?**

- **Does he or she have "stage presence"?**

- **Can the student think on his or her feet and bring the role to life?**

©1998 Good Apple                                           The Tempest **49**

# LET'S PUT ON A PLAY!

 Auditions can be intimidating and possibly embarrassing for many students. Instead of having them audition for the entire class, invite small student groups to audition different roles for the play. During tryouts, encourage students to offer encouragement and constructive criticism. "Can you look more at the audience?" is obviously better than "He never looks at the audience. He's terrible!" Before tryouts begin, discuss with students how to give constructive criticism in a kind, helpful, and respectful way. Write a list of rules on the board (e.g., *Be positive; Critique the "work," not the person;* and so on). As an alternative, invite students to write comments on note cards and give them to you. Read only those comments that are truly "constructive" and helpful to the performing student. Remind students that there is no one "right" way to do Shakespeare. A diversity of characterizations only adds dimension to the production. Invite groups to brainstorm each role and discuss their ideas with auditioning students.

*Critique the "work," not the person.*

 Even if your class is large, you can still get everyone involved in the production. Many students will want to act in the play, but some may prefer to work "behind the scenes."

Emphasize that *all* jobs are important to a production. Invite interested students to "apply" for the following jobs by writing a short paragraph about why they would be good at a particular task, or you can simply hold "interviews" with individual students. Encourage them to have first and second choices, so everyone has a chance to do something he or she enjoys.

## DIRECTOR
You may want to assume this responsibility, using one or two student assistants. The director helps place actors and scenery in the correct places, reminds actors when and how to project their voices, and keeps rehearsals structured. This is a difficult task, so make sure you choose students who aren't too "bossy." Many a production has crumbled because everyone resented the director's bossy ways.

## UNDERSTUDIES
Necessary only for the leading roles; if there is more than one performance, they may play the leads the second time.

## PROMPTER
Stands offstage during rehearsals and performances, and whispers lines and/or hints for the actors in case they forget their lines or where they should be onstage.

## STAGE MANAGER AND ASSISTANT
Ensure that production is going smoothly and all scenery and props are in place.

## MAKEUP ARTISTS
Decide on and apply makeup to actors before performances. (You may want to have two or three students for this job.) Call local cosmetology schools or colleges with theater departments for help.

# LET'S PUT ON A PLAY!

**COSTUMERS**
Research the time period in which the play takes place, and create costumes from available materials. (Ask parents to donate old clothes and fabric scraps.) Simple costumes such as tunics can be made from large shirts cinched with belts, and sweatpants can be pulled up to look like Renaissance-period pants.

**LIGHTING SPECIALIST**
Works with the director to manipulate lighting for dramatic effects.

**CURTAIN SPECIALIST**
Raises and lowers the curtain at the appropriate times.

**SCENERY AND PROP CREW**
Finds and/or makes appropriate scenery and props for the play, sets up and takes down scenery during performances, and cleans the stage and "theater" after performances.

**ADVERTISING AND PUBLICITY CREW**
Makes posters advertising the play. If you're inviting the whole school, write ads about the play and have them announced over the school intercom. If your production is going to be even larger, you might consider advertising it in your local newspaper or on your local public-access channel.

**PLAYBILL WRITERS AND ILLUSTRATORS**
Design and write a simple playbill with short blurbs about Shakespeare, the play, actors, scenes, and so on. This will add a nice dimension to your production.

**TICKET TAKER**
Necessary if you have parents coming to the performances. Most school plays are free, but you can "sell" tickets in exchange for a can of food for a local homeless shelter, a can of pet food or supplies for a local animal shelter, or other charitable donations.

**USHERS**
Show people to their seats and make certain "unruly" students keep quiet during performances.

**VIDEOGRAPHER**
Videotapes performances. This is great not only for critiquing the play later, but also authenticates the experience for students. They will love watching themselves on television. You may even want to make copies for families and friends to keep!

©1998 Good Apple

# JOURNAL/DISCUSSION TOPICS

To inspire students to think critically and form opinions, offer several of the following journal topics for discussion, reflection, and writing.

## ∞ ACT ONE ∞

▦ Miranda is moved to tears as she watches the great tempest destroy the ship at sea. She sympathizes with the ship's passengers even though she has never met them. Many times while we watch the news, television shows, or hear a story of someone going through a crisis, we too feel sorrow and pity. Tell about a story that disturbed or saddened you even though it didn't change or touch you personally. Why do you think such tragedies affect our emotions? Do you think it makes us better, more caring human beings? What do Miranda's tears say about her character?

▦ Prospero informs us that Ariel was "too delicate" to act out Sycorax's commands. What kind of demands do you think Sycorax made of Ariel? Write an imaginary "to-do" list which Sycorax might have given Ariel. Then discuss why you believe this list was too "vile" for the gentle spirit.

▦ Caliban dismisses Prospero's schooling, saying his only profit in learning language is that he knows "how to curse." Explain what you think Caliban means by this bitter statement. Has Prospero's teachings benefitted Caliban or do you think he would be better off if Prospero had never come to the island? Support your answer with reasons and ideas.

▦ Prospero is determined to make Ferdinand struggle for the love of the princess, "lest too light winning make the prize light." Do you believe that working for something makes the "prize" more valuable? Or do you think things handed over easily are just as important? Write about a time you worked hard to achieve something or to save for a desired item. Was the result worth the hard work?

# JOURNAL/DISCUSSION TOPICS

## ∞ ACT TWO ∞

▨ As soon as Miranda and Ferdinand see each other, they immediately fall in love. In fact, one of the first things Ferdinand says as he looks at the princess is "If your affections belong to no other, I'll make you the queen of Naples." What do you think of love at first sight? Is it only for fairy tales or does it happen in real life? What advice would you give this starry-eyed couple?

▨ As Gonzalo and Adrian discuss the enchantments of the island with Antonio and Sebastian, it seems as though the men are observing two separate places. Gonzalo believes it "lush" and "green" while Antonio scorns it as "tawny." Adrian finds the air sweet, while Sebastian sneers at the island's "rotten lungs." How can one place be seen in two very different ways? What does our attitude have to do with how we see the world? Look around a familiar place like your back yard or the school quad. Write two descriptions of that place from two different viewpoints. Write your first description as a pessimist might, finding only negatives, and then follow with an optimistic viewpoint, finding only positives. What can we tell about these men from their differing descriptions?

▨ Gonzalo fantasizes of a dream society where there is no poverty, felony, or violence. He imagines a world where everyone would live with nature's "abundance." Describe your vision of a dream society, including how the government would be run and how the people would live. Make a list of rules for your country for the citizens to live by. How does your world compare and contrast to Gonzalo's?

▨ "All the infections that the sun sucks up from bogs and swamps, on Prospero fall, and give him a disease!" curses Caliban. With a partner, list several gross or vile things found in nature. Think of animals, insects, molds, and other things you find disgusting. Referring to your list, write curses for Caliban to growl at Prospero. What would Caliban wish those foul items to do to Prospero? Share your "curses" with the class and vote on which is the most colorful, imaginative, and funny.

# JOURNAL/DISCUSSION TOPICS

## ACT THREE

🕮 Ferdinand tells Miranda that she makes his "labors pleasures." Sometimes hard work can be very pleasurable. Write about a time when you worked extremely hard on something, but it was actually very enjoyable. What is the difference between that and boring, painful labor? Compare your experience with Ferdinand's. Are there any similarities? Ferdinand's goal in working hard is to win Miranda's hand. What was the goal of your hard work? Did you achieve it?

🕮 Miranda, having been raised on an island with no knowledge of the outside world, is honest and frank and thus plays no "love games." Do you think it's better to state your feelings up front as they happen or to hold back and think on them before expression? Give the pros and cons of each situation.

🕮 Imagine that you, like Miranda, were raised on an island with your only companions being your studies, one parent, and a spirit such as Ariel. While there would be many difficulties being raised in such an environment, there would also be advantages. Name the benefits of being raised in such a way. Consider what kind of woman Miranda has become. What message could Shakespeare be giving regarding the the rules and confinements of society? Is he perhaps saying that because Miranda is closer to nature that she is more "pure" than those "corrupted" by society? Give several examples to support your opinion.

🕮 Gonzalo compares guilt to a "slow-working poison" which will now begin to "bite" at Alonso, Sebastian, and Antonio. Who of the three seems the most riddled with guilt? Support your answer with opinions and examples from the play. Then, write about a time when you felt guilty about something you did. Did your guilt feel like a "poison"? Compare your actions and punishments with Alonso's and Antonio's.

54 The Tempest ©1998 Good Apple

# JOURNAL/DISCUSSION TOPICS

## ACT FOUR

◻ On Prospero's magical island, sometimes it is difficult to tell what is real and what is magic. List all the occurrences that happen because of magic and those that happen naturally. Are there any events that could make both lists? Which list is the longest? What do these lists say about the mood and atmosphere of the island? What do they say about how much Prospero controls what happens throughout the play? Explain how Prospero's magic has created something like a tempest on the island through confusion, spells, punishments, and mangled plots.

◻ Discuss the character of Caliban. Is he indeed a monster or do you feel he is reacting to what he sees as Prospero cheating him out of his land? List Caliban's bad qualities and good qualities. What bad things has Caliban done? Can any of these actions be justified? Explain your answer.

◻ Imagine that Stephano's, Trinculo's, and Caliban's murder plot succeeded, and Stephano has become king of the island. He makes Miranda his bride and proclaims Trinculo and Caliban his viceroys, or governors. How would the island change? What rules do you think King Stephano would make? Would Caliban remain a happy servant? What would happen to Miranda? How would the two viceroys get along?

◻ Prospero punishes Stephano, Trinculo, and Caliban by chasing them with spirit-driven hounds and by infecting them with cramps and convulsions. Do you think this an effective and just punishment? How would you have punished them for their murder plot and thievery?

# JOURNAL/DISCUSSION TOPICS

## ⌘ ACT FIVE ⌘

▦ Look up the word *ambition* and write what it means in your own words. Most people consider ambition to be a good thing. In *The Tempest*, however, Prospero claims that ambition has caused his brother to lose his "good nature." When is ambition good? When is ambition evil? Discuss all the characters in the play whose ambitions drive their actions. Add whether or not you think their ambitions are good or evil, and why.

▦ At the end of the play, Prospero finally forgives all those people who "wronged" him. Have you ever forgiven someone for something they did to you which hurt you a great deal? How did you find it in your heart to forgive him or her? How does it feel to forgive? Do you think Alonso, Antonio, and Sebastian deserve Prospero's forgiveness? Are all three truly sorry for their crimes? What would you do with these men if you were Prospero?

▦ Caliban assures Prospero that he will be "wise hereafter" and awaits Prospero's pardon. Do you think that "bad" children or even demi-monsters like Caliban are "born that way" or do you think they are taught "bad" behavior? Do you believe Caliban can be taught good behavior? Do you think Prospero will forgive Caliban as he has the others? Why do you think Caliban humbles himself in front of Prospero? Do you think he is truly sorry?

▦ Many people consider either Prospero or Caliban as the hero of *The Tempest*. What reasons would you give for making Prospero the hero? What reasons would you give for making Caliban the hero? What qualities does each of these characters have that make him a bad hero? Is there anyone else in the play you consider a hero? If so, tell who it is and why you feel he or she is heroic.

# EXTENSION ACTIVITIES

## RELATIONSHIP CHART

Prospero's relationship to the many characters in *The Tempest* may be confusing to some students. To help them "map out" the characters' relationships, have students create a Relationship Chart following these directions.

1. Write Prospero's name in the middle of a sheet of paper and color a symbolic shape around it. This shape should reflect Prospero's personality. (e.g., a star may represent Prospero's magic; blue may symbolize the tempest he creates.)

2. Likewise, place character names with corresponding colored shapes around "Prospero." The closer these character shapes are in proximity to "Prospero," the closer the relationship.

3. Draw lines connecting all character shapes first to Prospero and then to any other characters with whom they have a relationship. Write what that relationship is along the line.

## CREATE YOUR OWN DEMI-MONSTER!

Invite students to create a demi-monster using cutout magazine pictures of various human and animal parts and by adding their own artistic details. Have students glue the pieces together on a sheet of paper; invent and name their "beast"; and tell about his or her personality, including fears, hopes, likes, dislikes, desires, and dreams. After the class has shared their demi-monster descriptions, explain that their beast lives alone in an isolated place, and a powerful and intelligent magician has taken over their monster's land and he is now to remain under the laws of this wizard. On a separate sheet of paper, have students describe their monster's new life, including the positive and negative aspects. Then have students compare their monsters to Caliban—How are they alike? How are they different? Caliban was born of a witch. How did students' monsters come into the world? As an extension, invite student pairs to write a dialogue between their monsters and Caliban to perform for the class.

# EXTENSION ACTIVITIES

## "THE IDEAL SOCIETY" AUCTION

Divide the class into groups of four or five students. Explain that they will have the chance to create the perfect society, just as Gonzalo imagined his. List the following attributes on the board:

| | |
|---|---|
| cooperation | military strength |
| education | peace |
| freedom | romantic love |
| health | strong families |
| kindness | wealth |

Tell each group they have 500 points with which to bid in a silent auction. Students will be bidding on which quality or qualities they feel would best represent their "perfect society." They may bid all 500 points to be sure of getting one quality, or break up their points and bid on more than one. You will play auctioneer in order to determine the winning bids.

Then invite groups to write a proposal to Prospero, asking permission to buy his island and set up the new society based on their purchased attributes. Have students explain why their group is most deserving of the island, citing the "ideal" attributes they've purchased. Acting as Prospero, you may determine which proposal is the most convincing.

## SOCIETY CHART

Discuss with students the qualities they think make an "ideal society." List their ideas on the board. Next to this list, write Gonzalo's attributes for the perfect society (i.e., *no magistrate, monarchy, felony, guns, knives, poverty, wealth, or occupation; people should live from nature's abundance and be idle, pure, and innocent*). Have students compare the two lists. What do the lists have in common? How are they different? Next, extend the chart into three columns, and invite students to list attributes of the society in which we live today. How does it compare to students' "ideal" society? Ask students what they consider to be today's society's biggest problem. Invite student groups to discuss and develop one way they can help alleviate or eliminate that problem.

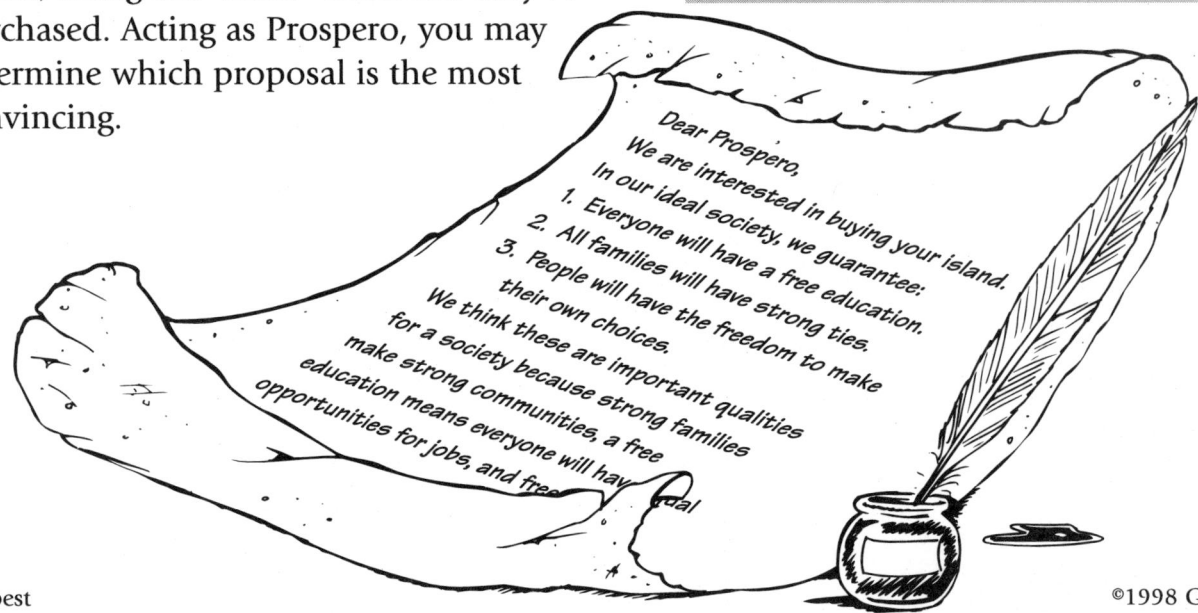

Dear Prospero,
We are interested in buying your island. In our ideal society, we guarantee:
1. Everyone will have a free education.
2. All families will have strong ties.
3. People will have the freedom to make their own choices.
We think these are important qualities for a society because strong families make strong communities, a free education means everyone will have opportunities for jobs, and free...

# EXTENSION ACTIVITIES

## THE BOOK OF MAGIC

Prospero achieves many feats of magic in *The Tempest*. He creates the tempest, music that places people under a spell, charms to turn Ariel into a harpy, magical goddesses who appear and reappear at will, and enchantments that disarm and weaken the strongest of men. In pairs, have students create a page from Prospero's book of magic. Each page should contain a "recipe" for the magic spell, including ingredients, directions, and an explanation of how the charm works and what it can do. Invite students to draw and label instructive and helpful pictures. Encourage them to be as creative as possible, and give examples of how the magic has been effectively demonstrated by either Prospero or Ariel. Bind the pages together into a class book of magic!

## THE MAGICAL MUSIC OF ARIEL

Invite students to create a CD cover for the magical music of Ariel. The cover should include: a title, picture, list of featured songs, magical elements each song may produce, inventive production label, and acknowledgements and thank-yous from the reigning artist, Ariel. As an extension, bring in an assortment of songs or excerpts you feel sounds lyrical and magical. Invite students to brainstorm what magic these songs might produce, and then invite them to bring in their own "magical music."

## WELCOME TO THE TWENTIETH CENTURY!

Imagine that Miranda, after being trapped on an island for 12 years, has been transported to modern times. In order to help Miranda survive life in the twentieth century, invite students to create a packet of helpful materials. Items may include an advice column of "dos" and "don'ts" for love, romance, and relationships in today's society; a picture dictionary of important 1990s technology; a map of your city or school, citing places of interest for young people; flash cards with modern slang on one side and their definitions and parts of speech on the other; and critiques on fashion, movies, and restaurants.

Discuss with students how Miranda might get by in this "brave new world" and the differences between her life on the island and life in modern times. Ask students if they think Miranda would be happier in our society or in her own, and explain why.

# EXTENSION ACTIVITIES

**REPORTING THE GOSSIP**

Have students pretend that they are reporters for Milan's premiere gossip column. After viewing several newspaper "gossip columns," invite students to write their own. They may wish to cover Miranda's and Ferdinand's wedding, the storm and shipwreck, any of the murder plots, Caliban's claims to the island, Prospero's magic, and so on. Students can compile their columns into a "gossip rag" and share them with the class.

**ISLAND TRAVEL BROCHURES**

Have students create travel brochures for the the magical island depicted in *The Tempest*. Before they begin, provide sample travel brochures for students to browse. Invite them to include the following elements in their brochures: "photos" (drawn or cut from magazines) and descriptive copy, including opportunities for outings, special features, modes of transportation, places to stay, and so on; names of talented tour guides and their experience (i.e., Ariel, Caliban, Miranda); testimonials from satisfied travelers who had a wonderful time on the magical island; and amazing, "unexpected" events that may occur.

***THE TEMPEST* REVIEW**

Show students examples of newspaper movie reviews and discuss the writing style. Then invite students to write reviews of the play following these directions.

1. Attach a real (or drawn) picture of yourself to a piece of paper, and write your name, grade, and school.

2. Begin your review with one descriptive word such as *exciting* or *funny*. Write a review of the play, including reasons why you chose that particular word.

3. Explain what you believe to be the best and worst aspects of the play.

4. Choose a character you like and one you dislike. Give reasons for your choices and how these characters affected you.

5. Give the play a grade such as A—*Outstanding*, B—*Good*, C—*Okay*, D—*A bomb!*

# EXTENSION ACTIVITIES

**CATEGORIES, CATEGORIES**

In groups of three, invite students to cut apart and sort these sentences, and place them in one of the following categories: *Early Milan, Takeover of Milan, Early Life on the Island, Developing Relationships, Punishment for Crimes,* or *Plans for the Future.* Students may debate which strip belongs under which heading, stimulating discussion and allowing them to revisit the text. Then, invite students to choose one sentence from each category that best summarizes the story.

Prospero creates a tempest.
Prospero begins to study his books.
Sycorax confines Ariel to a tree.
Caliban attempts to attack Miranda.
Sailors leave Sycorax behind.
Miranda and Ferdinand fall in love.
Ariel changes into a harpy.
Miranda is born.

Alonso believes his son is drowned.
Trinculo hides under Caliban's cape.
Ariel confines Alonso, Antonio, and Sebastian in a lime grove.
Gonzalo furnishes a boat with books and necessities.
Prospero turns hounds on Caliban, Trinculo, and Stephano.
Prospero invites everyone into his home to amaze them with his story.
Ferdinand must carry wood.
Prospero frees Ariel from the pine.
Prospero allows Antonio to act as duke in his place.
Caliban and Stephano plan to murder Prospero.
Prospero creates a masque of spirits to entertain Miranda and Ferdinand.
Antonio and Sebastian plot murder.
Prospero forgives his brother, Alonso, and Caliban.
Caliban desires a new master, Stephano.
An evil nature awakens in Antonio.
Miranda is tended by four or five women.
Prospero tells Miranda the story of how they came to the island.
Prospero teaches Caliban language.
Alonso confesses his guilt.
Alonso agrees to take double taxes if Antonio is made duke.
Prospero teaches Miranda.

# EXTENSION ACTIVITIES

**TEMPEST STEP BOOKS**

Write on the board: *First, Second, Next, Then,* and *Finally*. Give each student three sheets of drawing paper. Have them fold the first sheet approximately one-fourth from the top; the second about one-third from the top; and the third almost in half, leaving a 1" (2.5-cm) flap. Invite students to write sentences that retell the story of the *The Tempest*, beginning with *first, second, next, then,* and *finally*. Have students create step books, writing a sentence on each "flap" (see illustration). Have them draw a picture on each page of their books, illustrating the idea(s) presented in the sentence. Invite students to make a colorful cover and display books around the room.

**PROSPERO ON TRIAL**

Have two small student groups write scripts for a court case between Caliban and Prospero. One group consists of the "prosecuting attorneys," and the other "the defense." As the plaintiff, Caliban claims he is the original and rightful owner of the island and wants all rights and privileges of it. The defense must defend Prospero, explaining why he "took" the island. The defense could argue that Prospero "rescued" Ariel and Caliban, and improved civilization through means such as education. Encourage students to make their arguments as convincing as possible. You may act as judge, and invite the rest of the class to act as a jury, deciding which group presents the best argument.

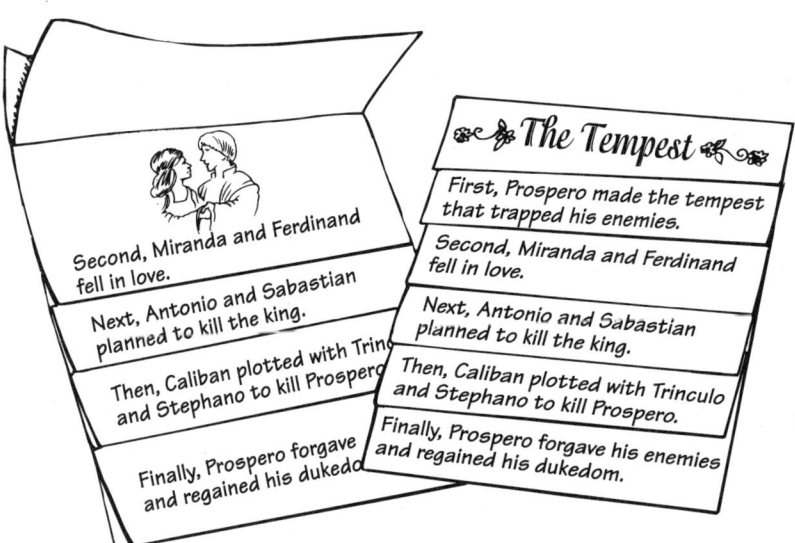

**WANTED!**

Invite students to create a "wanted" poster for Caliban, the mischievous and disgruntled demi-monster. Have them include a "photo," a list of his criminal activities (e.g., attacking Miranda, plotting to kill Prospero and take back the island, drinking "celestial" liquor, and so on), physical description, aliases, where he was last seen, his probable whereabouts, and any rewards being offered. Discuss with students who in the play might want to capture Caliban to keep him from committing more "crime." What punishment might he receive if he were captured? Students may also choose to create a "wanted" poster for other characters in the play, including Stephano, Alonso, Sebastian, Antonio, and Ariel.

# EXTENSION ACTIVITIES

**IMPROMPTU PERFORMANCES**

After reading and discussing the summary of the play, divide students into seven or eight groups and distribute a summary to each. Have groups decide where they think the summary should be broken down into scenes. Depending on your class size, have groups each take responsibility for performing one or two scenes for the class. Invite groups to perform using their own interpretation and language. Students will enjoy using their own "lingo," and you will be amazed to see the play come to life with students' own words and emotions.

Before groups perform, have them write a short summary of the scenes for which they are responsible. For example:

**Scene One**—Alonso and his men are shipwrecked during the tempest Prospero magically creates. Prospero and Miranda watch from the shore.

**Scene Two**—Prospero tells Miranda the story of how they came to be on the island.

**Scene Three**—Prospero puts Miranda to sleep and calls to Ariel. When Ariel asks for freedom, Prospero reminds him how he freed him from the witch Sycorax. Prospero then commands Ariel to lure Ferdinand with magical music.

**Scene Four**—Ferdinand and Miranda meet and instantly fall in love, which is part of Prospero's plan. Prospero accuses Ferdinand of being a spy.

**Scene Five**—The king and his men search for Ferdinand, but finally decide he must be drowned. Gonzalo then muses about his ideal society. Ariel puts everyone to sleep, except Sebastian and Antonio, who then plot the king's death.

**ALPHABET COUPLETS**

Assign student pairs two concurrent letters of the alphabet. Invite them to write and illustrate an alphabet couplet reviewing any theme, character, or object/prop in the play. When they are finished, display the couplets around the room for an instant play review! For example:

*A is for Ariel,*
*A spirit of the air.*
*B is for Books,*
*Prospero studies magic with care.*
*C is for Courage,*
*Ferdinand works with a plan.*
*D is for Demi-monster,*
*Caliban is half monster, half man.*

# EXTENSION ACTIVITIES & REFERENCES

## AGREE/DISAGREE

*The Tempest* contains many morals, lessons, and opinions about life. Invite students to think about these issues as an introduction to the play. Before reading the play, write the following statements on the board.

*I believe in love at first sight.*

*My parents understand more about love and relationships than I do.*

*I would be willing to forgive someone who betrayed me.*

*Revenge is sometimes a good way to resolve a problem.*

*It's okay to manipulate people into doing what you want.*

*It's good to be open and honest with feelings of love.*

*People should be forgiven no matter what they do.*

*It's okay to control those weaker than ourselves.*

Have students write *Agree* or *Disagree*, responding to each statement. Ask them to add one or two sentences explaining their answers. After they finish, read each statement aloud and ask students to raise their hands to show how they voted. Discuss these issues as a class—they should generate animated and lively debates. After you have studied the play, ask students to review the statements to see if they would change any of their answers. Then have them answer the questions from the perspective of a character in the play.

## REFERENCES

Coxwell, Margaret J. "Shakespeare for Elementary Students," *Teaching PreK–8* 27, no. 8 (March 1997): 40–42.

Durband, Alan, ed. *Shakespeare Made Easy: "The Tempest."* New York: Barron's, 1985.

Epstein, Norrie. *The Friendly Shakespeare.* New York: Viking, 1993.

Hillegass, L. L. *Cliffs Notes on Shakespeare's "The Tempest."* Lincoln, Nebraska: Cliffs Notes, Inc., 1971.

*The Illustrated Stratford Shakespeare.* London: Chancellor Press, 1982.

Onions, C. T. *A Shakespeare Glossary.* New York: Oxford University Press, 1986.